How to use this book

The drawings in this book have been made for you to trace, carbon, reverse, copy and enlarge. They are not intended for cutting out or to be displayed from the book.

Most of the drawings are simple enough to make tracing, copying and enlarging easy.

The figures in the section on ACTION POSES (Book 1) wear a plain robe so that their body position can be seen clearly. When you have studied the sections on CLOTHES (Book 1) and CHARACTERS (Book 2), you can dress your selected action figures in the appropriate attire, or alter the costumed figure to the pose required.

The INDEX will help you to choose the figures you need. Basic characters and age studies have been drawn so you will find that one figure will serve for several characters.

Always colour your visual aids. For backgrounds, see the hints given under the heading EASY BACKGROUNDS. For figures, the best results are painted on with coloured drawing inks. Coloured pencils and fibre tip pens are quicker and easier to use but do not give such neat or striking results. Use orange paint or ink watered-down, if you cannot get a flesh coloured crayon or pen.

Identification of story characters by colour is an effective method when using simple or silhouette figures. Use a light colour (yellow, cream or white) for Jesus's robe, and darker colours for other characters. Keep reds and purples for royalty, soldiers and officials or the key characters in your story. Women generally wore a blue dress and white headdress. Plain robes can be varied by drawing on coloured borders or braids, or by making the material striped.

Make use of the backgrounds shown. Most of them have suggested figures to use with them. By tracing several figures onto them you can build up a good frieze or picture. Use the notes and suggestions on the following pages, and try to be inventive. By moving your tracing paper about, part of one figure can be used with part of another. Rearrange faces, arms and legs to suit what you need.

Falcon Books

Contents

Book 1

HOW TO USE THIS BOOK
KNOW-HOW PAGES
ARRANGEMENT OF ILLUSTRATIONS
INDEX (ALPHABETICAL)
ACTION POSES: 1–80
CLOTHES: 81–110

Book 2

HOW TO USE THIS BOOK
CHARACTERS: 111–197
TRADES AND RECREATIONS: 198–246
OCCUPATIONS: 247–290
TRANSPORT: 291–301

Book 3

HOW TO USE THIS BOOK
PLANTS AND CREATURES: 302–404
BUILDINGS AND BACKGROUNDS: 405–440
LIST OF ILLUSTRATIONS (NUMERICAL)

Know-how pages

Tracing
Carboning
Reversing
Enlarging
Combining
Making and using templates
Stand-up card figures
Easy backgrounds
Use of colour
Collage
Flannelgraphs
Friezes

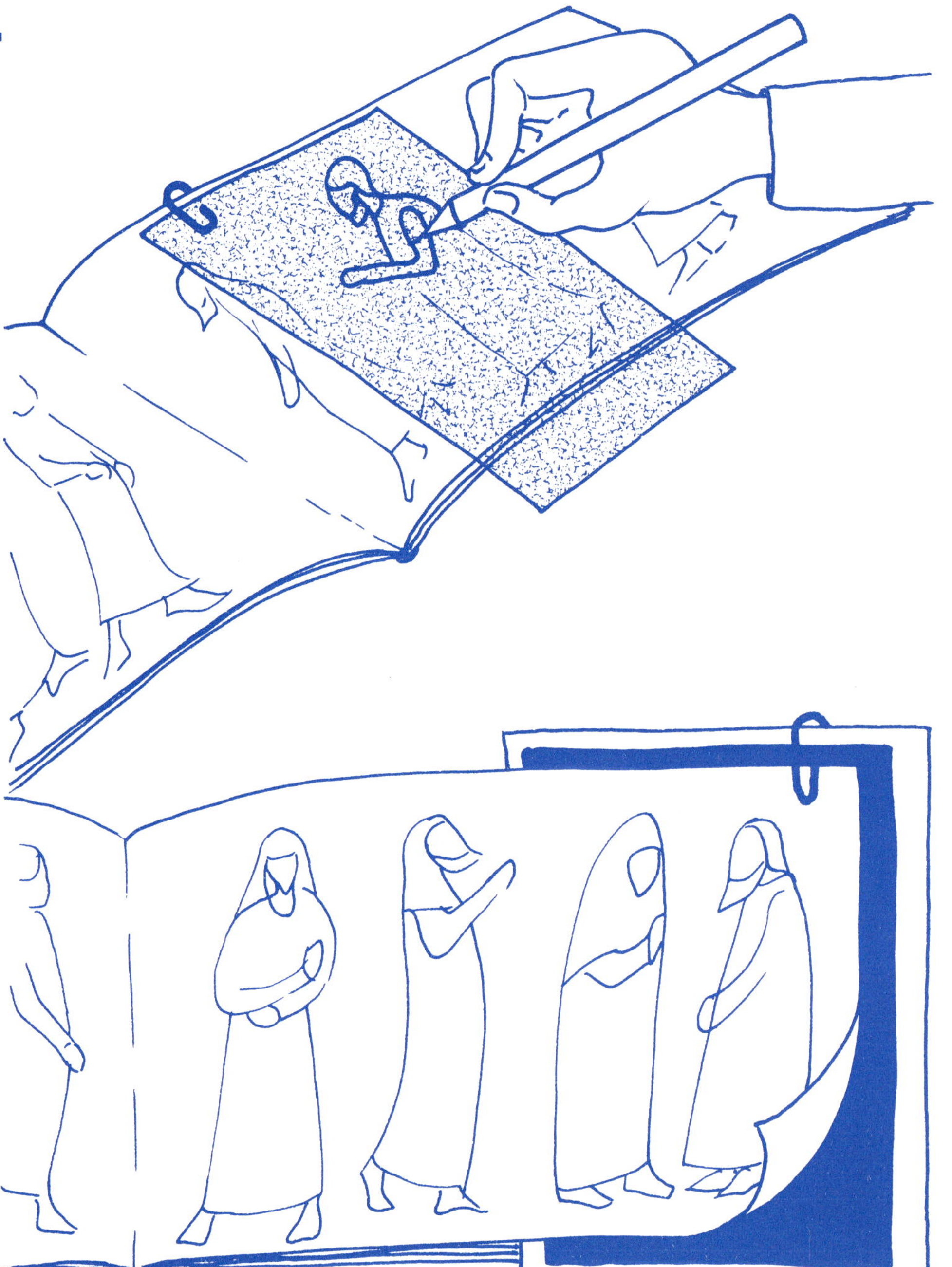

TRACING

Use tracing paper (or greaseproof, detail or any really thin paper) and a pencil. Select your picture or figure, place tracing paper over it and secure with a paperclip. Trace over the lines carefully. Remove the tracing paper and place it face down on a piece of scrap paper. Trace over the back of your design with a soft pencil or scribble over the entire area. Now clip the tracing paper, the first way up, on your plain paper or card. Trace carefully over the first lines again. Remove the tracing paper and draw over the traced lines neatly.

CARBONING *(Beware of smudging!)*

For quick, accurate results, place a sheet of carbon paper face down on a sheet of plain paper or card immediately under the selected picture. Trace over the design lightly with a pencil, dry ballpoint pen or stylus. Remove the carbon sheet and traced picture. Draw over carbon lines carefully, resting your writing hand on a piece of scrap paper to avoid smudging the carbon lines.

REVERSING

If you want your picture or figure to face the other way, use tracing paper and a pencil. Trace once, turn over the tracing paper onto plain paper or card. Trace over the back of the design, pressing firmly. Remove tracing paper. The reversed picture should have appeared faintly on the plain paper or card. Draw over it neatly.

ENLARGING

Any picture in this book can be enlarged quite simply if the following process is followed. Choose a simple figure first if you have never done this before.

With a pencil and ruler, draw horizontal and vertical lines across the page or picture all 1 cm apart. This divides the page into 1 cm squares. On the paper or card on which you need your enlarged picture, draw these lines all over again, but making them 2 cm apart, so your paper is divided into 2 cm squares. (This will make the picture twice as big as the original. If you want it even bigger, draw your lines further apart. 3 cm squares will make your picture three times as large, 4 cm squares four times as large *etc*. Should you wish to reduce a picture, reverse the process.) Enlarge the picture one square at a time, *ie*. draw everything you see in small square 1A in large square 1A, and so on, until you have a complete replica of the small picture. Rub out the squares on the large drawing carefully and finish off the picture or figure. *This is not an easy process, but you will improve with practice*. The accompanying pair of figures show you how to enlarge to approximately twice the size (double the height and width, *ie*. four times the area). Try to complete the larger figure for practice.

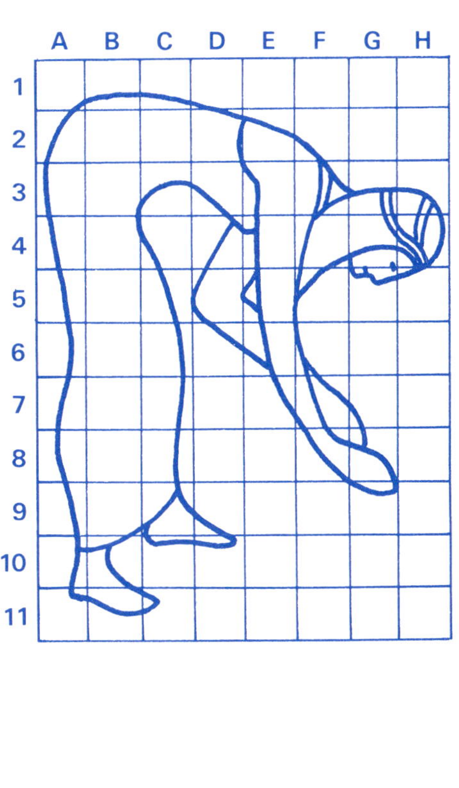

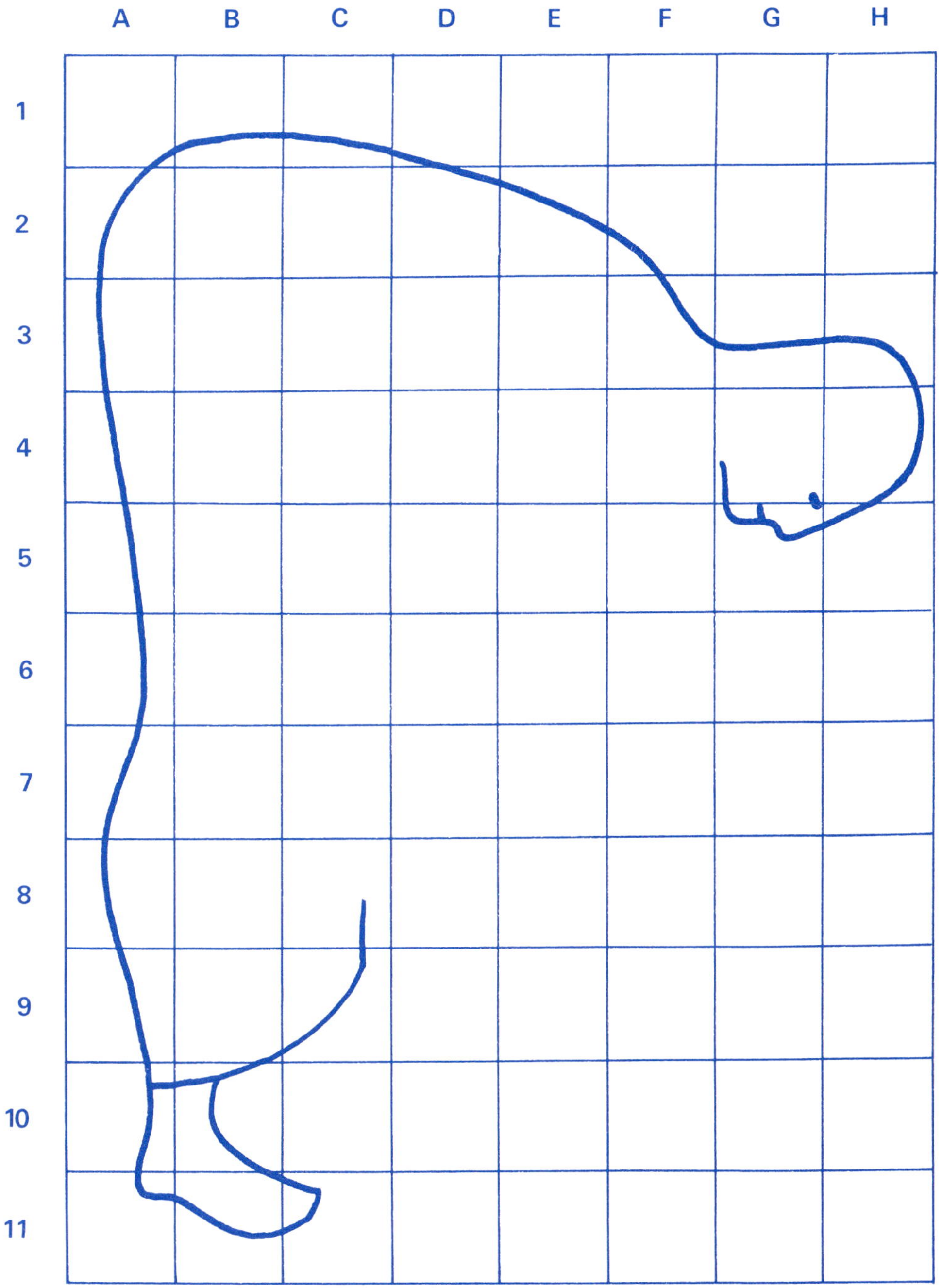

A know-how page

COMBINING

This is a more complicated process than plain tracing or copying but it will become easier with practice. If the figure you require can only be obtained by combining two or more figures, for instance the head of one with the body of another, trace only the part of the first figure that you require, remove the tracing paper, then put it down onto the second figure and complete the tracing. Your finished figure is then a combination of both. The same method can be used to make figures bend over or have arms or legs in different positions. Trace the part of the figure that you want, then move the tracing paper fractionally and the body, arm or leg can be drawn at a slightly different angle to the original. The series of drawings of fishermen (Figures 279–284) will need to be used with the fishing boat (294) so use this method of combination tracing. There are other figures which need to be matched together in this way—the INDEX will tell you which they are.

KNOW-HOW PAGES

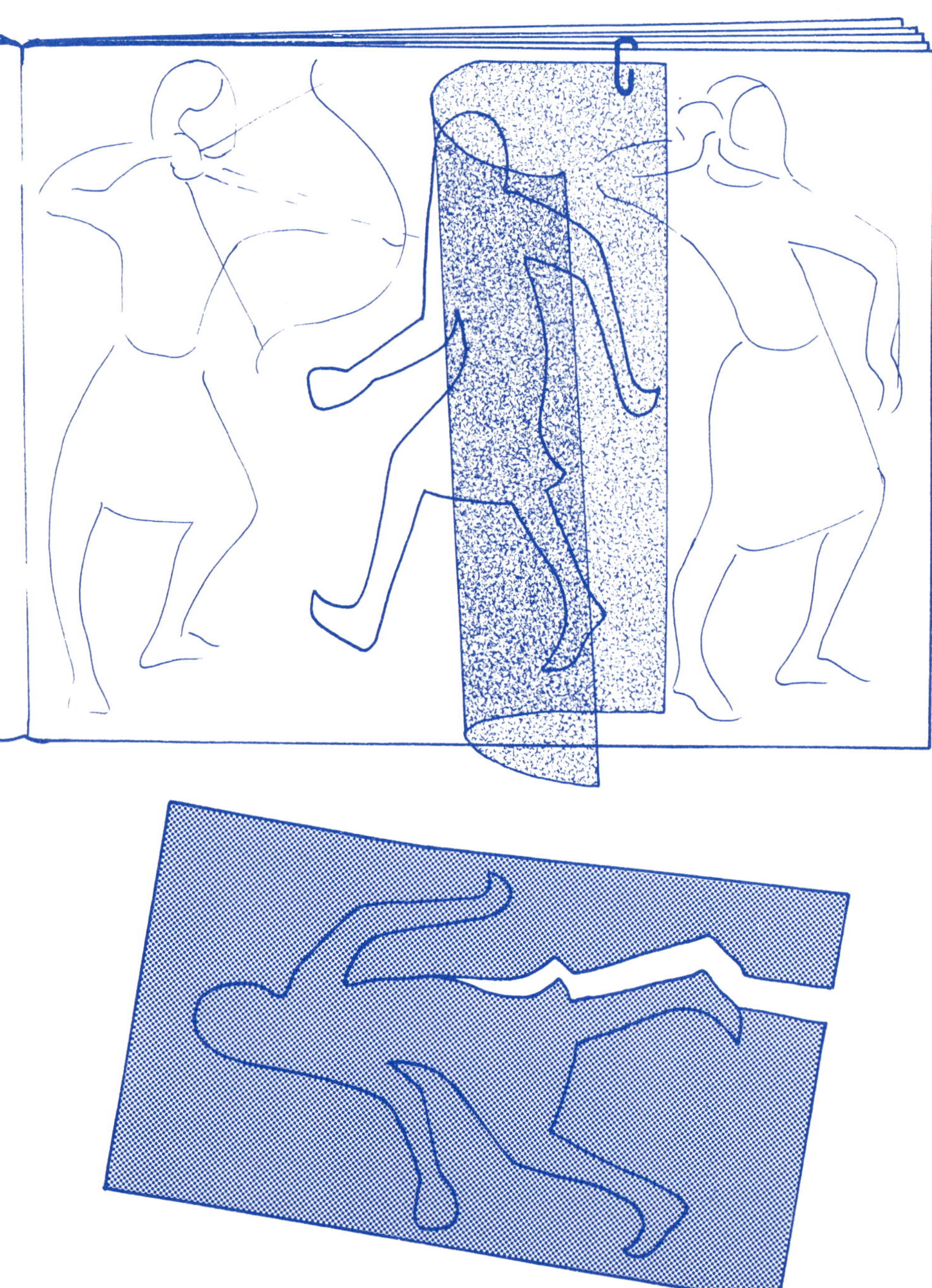

MAKING AND USING TEMPLATES

Templates help teachers and children to draw shapes of people, animals, birds, trees, houses *etc.* with speed and accuracy.

Make a template by selecting your shape, tracing it onto card and cutting it out. Use the tracing paper or carbon method and remember about reversing and enlarging.

The teacher can make great use of these templates when preparing cloth, plain paper, gummed paper and blotting paper shapes for friezes and flannelgraphs. Use the comprehensive INDEX to help you find suitable figures. Choose a simple shape which will be recognisable in silhouette so that the other details can be omitted where necessary.

Templates made for children to use are valuable since 'activity time' is often brief and good results are necessary to keep enthusiasm. A child of any age being given a template can begin by drawing or cutting out a good basic shape—often unobtainable freehand. It can then be coloured in and form part of a worthwhile picture or figure for the frieze.

For figures on which children are required to fill in facial features, use *front facing figures* only. Children have been proved unable to put profile features onto profile faces. Front facing features on profile faces do look rather strange! This is why very few of the faces in this book have definite profiles.

STAND-UP CARD FIGURES

Make card figures as described under MAKING AND USING TEMPLATES. To colour quickly and effectively, completely cover the figure with a rectangular piece of coloured gummed paper. Stick it onto one surface, turn it over and trim off the excess round the edge of the card. Cover the head, hands and feet with pieces of flesh coloured gummed paper, trim round. Cover the top of the head with another colour gummed paper for hair or hat and trim off excess. For a female shape cover the head area with one colour, trim, stick a round shape over the top.

To stand figures on a polystyrene tile fix a cocktail stick or sharpened match to the back of the ready coloured figure with adhesive tape, leaving 0·5 cm showing below the base of the figure so that it can be pushed into the polystyrene. Animals and some objects can also be made to stand on the tile by this method. Anything too tall will overbalance the tile which is very light unless it is mounted on a heavy block.

For figures to stand in slots or fit into slits on card backgrounds allow an extra 3 or 4 cm on the base of the figure before cutting it out of the card. Snip and taper the bottom corners of the tab. Colour the figure only, as the card tab will be hidden.

For free standing figures, colour as already described. Make a card hinge $\frac{2}{3}$ the height and $\frac{2}{3}$ width of the figure. Crease the top quarter of the hinge and glue it onto the back of the figure.

To simulate walking, make and colour a large *profile* figure down to the hem of the long robe. Make a card disc with its diameter a little less than the width of the base of the robe. Onto the disc stick four identical feet and ankles spacing the feet evenly round the circumference and with the ankles meeting at the centre. Fix the disc behind the base of the robe with a brass-headed paper clip through the centre. The wheel will move round as you push it along.

A know-how page

EASY BACKGROUNDS

Pictures and friezes are often spoilt by poor backgrounds. The method described here is quick and effective. Good backgrounds are important. Useful layouts which can be made by this method are shown on the following pages.

Always try to build your background onto coloured paper as white is seldom suitable and, if used, requires more skill, time and materials to produce a good result. Children will become easily discouraged if their frieze is not attractive or is made by a poor method. Time for this activity is often short and the quick methods described here can be usefully employed. Use figures made by templates which can be added to the finished background.

Coloured sugar paper is good to use for backgrounds and can be purchased from art shops. To save expense, keep old wallpaper, plain coloured paper bags and plain wrapping paper. These can be used successfully and cost nothing. If you are more adventurous, collage pictures can be made from fabric scraps and other waste materials in a similar way. See the notes on COLLAGE.

Begin your background with blue paper if you can, as it will show for the sky (also sea, lake, river if needed).

From another colour cut the skyline silhouette, for example, green or mauve for hills, and stick it onto the blue. Cut the next layer of the landscape from a contrasting colour, for example, yellow or brown for the beach or desert and stick it immediately below the previous layer. Finish off with some grey and black foreground, for rocks. Over this total background can be pasted trees, houses, people, animals, all in silhouette. Old wallpaper can be used as a base for a long frieze but add the background as described above.

Flannelgraphs can be built up in a similar way using coloured blotting paper for the different silhouettes placed on a cloth background (see notes on FLANNELGRAPHS). You will not be able to place figures *etc.* over other blotting paper shapes, so plenty of space for the action part of your story must be left as cloth. A line of hills or a few trees will help to set the scene for your figures and animals.

USE OF COLOUR

Always colour your visual aids. The drawings in this book are not intended to be used as they are. They have been made simple for ease of copying, leaving plenty of scope for the imaginative worker to add detail and interest. There is no need to make such a thick outline; just trace your chosen figure in pencil and colour each area as you would pictures in a child's painting book. Read about quick ways for colouring backgrounds under the heading EASY BACK-GROUNDS, and for card figures under MAKING AND USING TEMPLATES.

The best results are obtained by painting with coloured drawing inks, as these are transparent and vivid. Coloured pencils and fibre tipped pens are easier to use but do not give such a striking or neat result. Water colour paints are more difficult to use unless you are very experienced. Flesh colour is hard to obtain. Use orange paint or ink watered down rather than red or pink. Alternatively try and purchase a flesh coloured crayon or pen.

Palestinian women generally wore blue robes with a white headdress. Men's robes can be varied by drawing on coloured borders or braids or by making the material striped. The poorer people wore coarse material in neutral colours (homespun) and the rich would have purchased fine weave cloth which had been dyed. Plain garments were often decorated, particularly the women's robe which had traditional brightly coloured embroidery on a panel at the neck. A touch of silver or gold makes royalty,

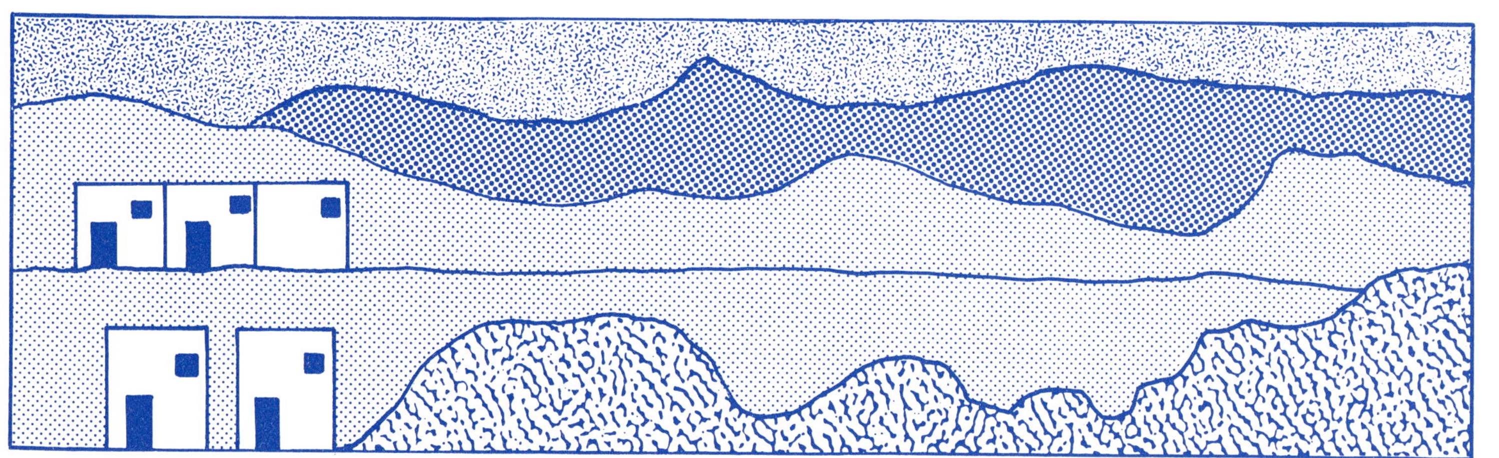

jewelry, armour and weapons more special.

Identification of story characters by individual colours is an effective method when using simple or silhouette figures. Use a light shade (yellow, cream or white) for Jesus's robe and darker colours for other characters. Keep reds and purples for royalty, soldiers and officials, or the key character in your story. You will find that children will quickly identify even the most simple shape if you remain constant in your use of colours throughout the story.

If you are using a scenic background, try to build your picture on coloured paper rather than white. Blue sugar paper is good for this. It immediately gives depth and is of course ideal for suggesting both sky and sea. For a change, try to introduce texture by making your backing sheet or figures out of wallpaper or fabric (see also the notes on COLLAGE).

Gold, silver or coloured foil used occasionally can be most attractive, particularly for small children, and will add a hint of something special to a story. For instance, stick red foil flames on the burning bush (317) or Elijah's altar (434) on Mount Carmel. A heap of silver fish (374) covered with a net bag can bring Luke 5 to life. Then it is possible to make the Ark (431) or Solomon's Temple (422) out of gold foil. Animal silhouettes also lend themselves to being made out of fabric. A camel or horse cut out of brown flannel or a sheep from cotton wool or lint becomes much more lifelike.

COLLAGE

Pictures made up from junk materials are effective and fun to do, especially for children under ten years of age. These pictures can have an added dimension and help children to appreciate detail. In this way, they often remember more from the stories. Research has shown that children retain 90% of what they *do*, in contrast to 10% of what they hear and 50% of what they see.

Base
Use tough paper (the back of old wallpaper glued double) or a large sheet of card. Flower boxes are ideal and are often given away by florists.

Glue
Brown glue is strong but very sticky. It might be better to limit its use to the older children. Pour a little into plastic pots and spread with paste brushes. For very young children, mix up wallpaper paste very thickly so that it will not spill, and allow the picture to dry overnight before attempting to move it. Obstinate materials such as plastic net, tinfoil and polystyrene may need to be stuck with a rubber or plastic solution. Do not let children use this themselves as it will not come off clothes and is too expensive to be used wastefully.

Materials
A few suggestions to begin with: ▶

Coloured magazines
These can be torn into small pieces of separate colours and pasted on rather like a mosaic. Older children enjoy this and can do it well.

Storage
Successful collage means the continuous salvaging of any interesting household rubbish. Storage is frequently a problem and you need to discover the most convenient and unobtrusive method for your home. It is usually impossible to gather instantly enough material for a collage, starting from scratch, so store your finds systematically and continuously. Cereal boxes and other empty cardboard cartons can have their sides and tops and bottoms cut off so that the useful faces can be stored flat.

Construction
Children are very inventive and are mostly used to this type of activity at school. Give them plenty of varied materials and a little guidance and they will enjoy it. You may like to draw on a silhouette outline for the background using ideas from Figures 435–440. People, trees, animals and buildings can be made separately by the children using templates or shapes from the appropriate figures and then added on top of the background.

See examples on following four pages

Sea and sky	Net and chiffon fabric, crêpe and tissue paper, cellophane, tinfoil
Beach and roads	Brown paper, sand paper, textured wallpaper, sand, lentils, wood shavings, sawdust
Land and vegetation	Corrugated painted card, tweed and corduroy fabric, coloured paper, seed catalogues and covers, tubes (for tree trunks)
Buildings and boats	Match boxes, mini-cereal boxes, polystyrene, thick wallpaper, wood grain Fablon, net bags (for fishing nets)
People and animals	Checked and striped fabric, wool, fur, velvet, cotton wool, pipe cleaners

KNOW-HOW PAGES

A know-how page

A flannelgraph background can be made from any material that has some kind of pile. Felt or baize is the most hard wearing but is expensive compared with a piece of old blanket or flannelette sheet. Brightly coloured pieces of flannel can be bought from Bible book shops for flannelgraphs. Clip or pin the material to a board when in use or glue it to stiff card and store it flat.

The easiest way to make figures for a flannelgraph is by cutting silhouettes from coloured blotting paper (see the notes on USE OF COLOUR). Either draw round templates (see notes on MAKING AND USING TEMPLATES) or trace or carbon directly from this book onto the blotting paper and cut out the figures. Details can be drawn on with a felt pen or colour added to white shapes with wax crayon. The blotting paper method is quick and versatile as scenery, buildings, animals and figures can be made from the various colours. It can also be used for diagrams, quizzes and word flashes.

For more detailed figures, draw on a sheet of paper and glue this to a large sheet of blotting paper. When the glue is dry colour the figures. Finally cut them out. You may have to roughen the back of the blotting paper with a blade or sandpaper to make it stay on the background. Heavier or larger paper figures should be backed with squares of lint. Large card figures are better used on a teazelgraph. In this case, stick squares of 'velcro' or hooks on the figures and use a brushed nylon type fabric for the background.

FRIEZES

Attractive friezes can be made from coloured paper as described in the notes on backgrounds. Use a strip of wallpaper as a backing and prepare your basic scene before the class begins. This will ensure that the children have a good background on which to stick their figures. A large frieze need not be expensive, if you save plain coloured wrapping paper and bags and use these instead of coloured art paper.

Study the notes on COLLAGE to give you new ideas but you will probably find that gummed paper figures are the quickest and easiest method (see notes on MAKING AND USING TEMPLATES).

Arrangement of illustrations

ACTION POSES
1–27 Jesus and disciples
28–55 The sick and tired
56–77 Acts and emotions
78–80 Crowds

CLOTHES
81–110 Jewish costume

CHARACTERS
111–134 Faces and expressions
135–142 Young men and maidens
143–154 Children and old men
155–158 Angels or messengers
159–166 Kings and queens
167–182 Romans and Egyptians
183–189 Soldiers
190–197 Slaves and master

TRADES AND RECREATIONS
198–209 Musicians and instruments
210–223 Pots and potter
224–228 Scrolls and scribe
229–231 Trading
232–240 Carpentry
241–246 Child care

OCCUPATIONS
247–255 Women at work
256–258 Shepherds
259–264 In the fields
265–278 Baskets and carriers
279–284 Disciples fishing
285–290 Tax collection

TRANSPORT
291–298 Ships and sea
299–301 Overland

PLANTS AND CREATURES
302–355 Flowers and trees
356–376 Birds and fishes
377–385 Creeping things
386–404 Cattle and beasts

BUILDINGS AND BACKGROUNDS
405–420 Houses and tent
421–434 Synagogue and Temple
435–440 Mountain and valley

Index

A

AARON 152
AARON'S ROD see ALMOND
ABEDNEGO 87
ABEL (SLAIN) 54
ABRAHAM 151
ADAM 84
ADZE 233
AHAB (SULKING) 55
ALMOND blossom 332; branch 331; bud 333; fruit 335; tree 334; for Aaron's rod use 331–335
ALTAR of incense 429; of sacrifice 430; of stone 434; for Isaac use figure 54
AMOS 87
ANANIAS 81
ANEMONE/LILY (ANEMONE CORONARIA) 314
ANGEL OR MESSENGER announcing 157 (fits onto body 155—repeat for heavenly host); explaining 155; sitting 158 (also suitable for Abraham's visitors and Gideon's angel); with sword 156
ANGER 67
ANGRY (also see FACES) 68
ANISE, DILL OR FENNEL (ANETHUM GRAVEOLENS) 304
ANNA (PROPHETESS) 142
ANNAS (HIGH PRIEST) 106
ANNUNCIATION see ANGEL OR MESSENGER
ANOINTING 60
APPLE TREE see FRUIT TREE
AQUILA 87
ARCHER 75, 135
ARK see NOAH'S ARK
ARK OF THE COVENANT 431 (extend ends of carrying pole to fit shoulder and hands of Levites 107)
ARTAXERXES (KING OF PERSIA) 159
ARTEMIS (GODDESS DIANA OF EPHESIANS) 433
ASSES ass, mule or donkey 386 (carries rider 54, 243 or 248 reversed); donkey 387 (carries rider 21 or can be tethered); foal 388 (carries rider 24)
ASSYRIAN SOLDIER 188
ATHALIAH (QUEEN MOTHER) 163
AWL 237
AXE 234

B

BAAL 432
BABY being held 241; in manger 242; lying 245 (fits manger 242 and basket 270); sitting 243
BAG (OR PURSE FOR MONEY) 276 (kept in fold of shirt above belt 82)
BALANCE (SCALES FOR WEIGHING) 230
BAPTISM of Jesus 3; of man 85, 86; of woman 63
BARABBAS 169
BARNABAS 87
BASKETS for bread 271; for feeding of four thousand 273 (rope fish basket); for feeding of five thousand 267 (Jewish hamper 265–267—wicker food basket, capacity two gallons); for fish 273; for food (picnics) 265–267; for Paul's escape from Damascus 273; for produce 269 (storage basket); for storage 269; of reeds 270 (to fit baby Moses 245 cut slit along front rim); of rope 273; for carrying beads, clay, fruit, wool 268
BATTLE 74 (duplicate figures several times and dress in appropriate armour; see soldiers 183, 186–189)
BEACH 435
BEAKER 214
BEAUTIFUL GATE 424 (extreme left)
BED in use 35, 47–49; rolled up 36
BEGGAR 28, 30, 33
BENJAMIN 136
BENJAMIN'S SACK 278
BELSHAZZAR (KING OF BABYLON) 161
BELT FOR MONEY 274 (made from two strips of cloth joined at base and tied at waist, remainder being for decoration)
BENT WOMAN 41
BETHANY 413
BETHLEHEM street 409 (for crowds use 80); town 414
BIRDS cock 366; dove flying down at Baptism 360; hen 370; hen gathering chicks under wing 371; pigeon, rock dove 359 (for sacrifice, draw two); quails (18 cm long) 367–369; raven carrying meat 357; raven flying 358; raven standing 356; sparrows or sparrow-like birds 363–365; sold two for a penny or five for two pennies 362; turtle dove 361 (fit olive branch 338 in beak)

BLESSING (JESUS) bread 8; children 4
BLIND Bartimaeus 31; man or beggar 28
BLOSSOM see ALMOND
BLOWING SHOFAR (RAM'S HORN TRUMPET) 198
BOAT (FISHING, ON SEA OF GALILEE) 294, 295 (unfurled sail indicated by dots; continue sail and gaff of 294 upwards as in 295; for stormy water, fit waves 298 over waterline)
BOAZ 81
BOOK OF THE LAW see SCROLL / DECREE / EDICT
BOOTHS (FOR FESTIVAL OF TABERNACLES) see HERBS AND SPICES / myrtle
BOW DRILL 236
BOW SAW 239
BOWL 212
BOY David 145; Jesus 143; Samuel 146; Widow of Zarephath's son 150; general 144; with loaves and fishes 147
BRAMBLE/BRIAR (RUBUS ULMIFOLIUS) 318
BRANCHES (FOR BOOTHS) see HERBS AND SPICES / Myrtle
BREAD bread and wine 9; blessing bread 8; breaking bread 10; feeding five thousand 11; making bread 249
BREASTPLATE see HIGH PRIEST
BRIAR/BRAMBLE (RUBUS ULMIFOLIUS) 318
BROOK OF CHERITH see WILDERNESS
BUD see ALMOND
BUILDING Egyptian brick; slaves carrying bricks 195; carrying mud in basket 190; Egyptian task master 194; hoeing mud 192; moulding mud into bricks 196; pulling stone on sledge 191 (continue sledge); stacking bricks 197; tipping on water to mix mud 193
BULRUSHES/PAPYRUS (CYPERUS PAPYRUS) 322 (use base repeated along river bank)
BUNCH OF GRAPES see VINE (VITRIS VINIFERA)
BUNDLE OF FLAX (DRIED ON ROOFTOPS) 325
BURDEN BEARER 301
BURNING BUSH/THORN 317
BUSHEL 218

C

CAESAR (AUGUSTUS) 167
CAIAPHAS (HIGH PRIEST) 106
CAIN (KILLING ABEL) 69
CALF 389 (draw on base and stand for Golden Calf)
CALLING (JESUS) disciples 6; Zacchaeus 5
CAMEL sitting 404 (complete by tracing neck and head from camel 403); walking 403 (fit on figure or load from 404)
CAMEL HAIR CLOAK 92
CAMP see TENT (NOMADIC)
CANDLESTICK (SEVEN BRANCHED) 428
CARPENTER 232 (any tool fits right hand at angle drawn)
CARPENTRY TOOLS adze 233; awl 237; axe 234; bow drill 236; bow saw 239; chisel 238; hammer 235; saw 240
CARRYING baby 241; basket or load on shoulder 190; load or cross under left arm 86; lost sheep 257; pitcher 252, 255; weight 196 (alter object to fit)
CART 300 (omit hay load when carrying ark or people; fit black shaft to oxen 390)
CASTING NET 283
CATTLE calf 389 (draw on base and stand for Golden Calf); fat cow 391; cow sitting 389; thin cow 392; oxen 390 (fit black shaft to 263, 264, 300)
CAVE (INSIDE) 418 (use sleeping figure 52 and hiding figure 73)
CEDAR (CEDRUS LIBANI) of Lebanon (grows to 40 m) 352; branch 353
CENTURION 185 (holds spear in right hand)
CHARIOT 299 (pulled by horse 398 with Egyptian soldier 178 standing; reins tie round waist leaving hands free; for Philip and Eunuch, use Egyptian driver 177 and seated figures 18, 21; extend chariot 5 cm to left)
CHILDREN asking 143; being carried 150; kneeling 146; offering lunch 147; sick or sleeping 47; sitting 246; talking 144; throwing stone 145; toddler 244; with Jesus 4 (adapt as required)
CHISEL 238

CITY (ON HILL WITH WALL) Jerusalem, Jericho, Samaria 412 (reverse, using left hand dots as hinge)
CITY (STREET) 409 (crowd 80 fits street)
CLEANSED see LEPER
CLEOPAS (OR FRIEND) 87, 89
CLOAK 90 (owned by everyone, used as blanket at night; made from thick strip of woven cloth, wrapped around body, joined along shoulders with slits for arms)
CLOTHES see separate entries
COAT 89 (worn over shirt; wealthy people wore additional coat over first coat 89 instead of traditional cloak 90); coat over coat 89; long-sleeved coat 88, 137; special-occasions coat 104; working coat 87
COCK 366
COINS denarius 289; drachma 290; shekel 288
COLT 388 (carries rider 24)
CORN (TRITICUM COMPOSITUM) (variety of wheat with seven ears per stalk) ear of wheat 326; sheaves of corn 328; 327
COUCH 55
COURT of Gentiles 424 (Gentiles not allowed inside Temple); of Priests 424 (up first set of steps— see TEMPLE (HEROD'S)); of Women 423 (money chests kept in foreground)
COW see CATTLE
CROCUS/SAFFRON (CROCUS SATIVUS) 316
CROOK see SHEPHERD
CROPS see FLAX (LINUM USITATISSIMUM), CORN (TRITICUM COMPOSITUM) and VINE (VITRIS VINIFERA)
CROWD listening and watching 79 (fits hillside 437 and beach 435); sitting facing reader 78 (fits hillside 436 for feeding of five thousand); walking 80 (fits 440 for crossing Red Sea and 409 for crowded street)
CRYING see FACES
CUP see POTTERY
CURED see PARALYTIC (SICK OF THE PALSY)
CYCLAMEN (CYCLAMEN PERISCUM) 315
CYMBALS see MUSICIANS AND MUSICAL INSTRUMENTS

CYPRESS (CUPRESSUS SEMPERVIRENS) branch 354; tree (grows to 40 m) 355
CYRUS (KING OF PERSIA) 159

D

DAGON 432
DANIEL 82
DARIUS (KING OF PERSIA) 159
DATE PALM see PALM (PHOENIX DACTYLIFERA)
DAVID boy 145; young man 137 (*coat optional*); playing lyre 208; slaying Goliath 145
DEAD BODY lying in road 54; wrapped in grave clothes 50 (*omit bier*)
DEAF AND DUMB 29 (*fits waist 28*)
DEBORAH 140
DECREE/EDICT/SCROLL 224, 225
DELILAH 63
DEMETRIUS 169
DEMONIAC 39
DENARIUS 289
DENIAL 81
DESERT 436, 438
DIANA OF EPHESIANS 433
DILL/ANISE/FENNEL (ANETHUM GRAVEOLENS) 304
DISCIPLES asleep in garden 40, 73; fishing 279–284; reclining 16, 17; sitting 15; standing 81–83, 87, 88, 90, 151; stripped for work 84–86; travelling 148, 152
DISEASED bent woman 41; demoniac 39; man with dropsy 38; man with withered hand 37; sitting by pool 40
DONKEY/ASS/MULE 386
DORCAS 47, 171
DOVE 360
DRACHMA 290
DRAWING WATER see WOMEN AT WORK
DREAMING 52 (*for Jacob at Bethel*)
DRESS 103 (dress made like shirt 82, generally blue with traditional embroidery at neck; over was worn headdress 95, 96, 103 or shawl 102 and, for special occasions, coat 104)
DRINKING (AT MEAL) 17
DROPSY 38
DRUM 205

E

EAR OF WHEAT 326
EATING 12, 16
EBED-MELECH 175
EDICT/DECREE/SCROLL 224, 225
EGYPTIAN chariot 299; maidens 179, 180 (*lifting Moses 245 from basket 270*); Pharaoh 178; Pharaoh's daughter 181; Potiphar's wife 182; prince 176; princess 181; soldier 177; steward 175
ELDERS 110
ELI 149
ELIEZER 148
ELIJAH 82, 150
ELISHA 82
ELIZABETH 141
ELKANAH 151
EMMAUS 413
EPHOD see HIGH PRIEST
ESAU adult 152; young man 135
ESCAPING 76
ESTHER 164
EVE 63
EWES see SHEEP
EXODUS 80 (*use crowd walking*)
EZRA 105

F

FACES angry 133; crying 130; elderly 119–122; fat 123; happy 128; jeering 132; laughing 134; middle aged 113, 114, 117, 118; poor 126; rich 125; sad 129; shouting 127; smiling 128; sneering 132; thin 124; thinking 131; yawning 127; young 111, 112, 115, 116
FACE VEIL 97
FACE WRAPPED IN MANTLE 70
FARMING gleaning 261; ploughing 263 (*fit black shaft to oxen 390*); reaping 260; sowing 262; threshing 264 (*threshing board had iron or stone teeth on underside; thresher holds goad in right hand; fit black shaft to oxen 390*); winnowing 259 (*with fan or shovel*)
FATHER AND SON 58, 59 (*prodigal*)
FEEDING OF FIVE THOUSAND 11
FENNEL/ANISE/DILL (ANETHUM GRAVEOLENS) 304

FIELD 436
FIG (FICUS CARICA) fruit and leaves 340; tree (bushlike with several stems) 341
FIGHTING see BATTLE
FIR see PINE OR FIR (ALEPPO PINE, PINUS HALEPENSIS)
FISH barbel 373 (*30 cm long*); bleak/lake sardine (*20 cm long*) 374 (*often pickled and taken on picnics 147*); blue mullet (*50 cm long*) 375; St Peter's fish/talapia 372; *all plentiful in Sea of Galilee, so would have been caught by disciples*
FISHING letting-down nets 280; mending nets 281; pulling-in boat 279; pulling-in drag-net 284; pulling-in nets 282; standing near shore throwing cast net 283 (*use enlarged background 435*); all fit boat 294 for completion
FLAIL (FOR WINNOWING) 259
FLASK 210
FLAX (LINUM USITATISSIMUM) bundle of flax 325 (*dried on rooftops*); flower and plant 324 (*pulled up by roots for drying*); flower is bright blue
FLOOD 298 (*repeat by matching dots*)
FLUTE 204
FLY 384
FOAL see ASSES
FOOTWASHING 13, 14
FORTIFIED TOWN OR CITY see CITY (ON HILL WITH WALL)
FOUR FRIENDS 35 (*carrying paralytic*)
FRANKINCENSE (BOSWELLIA THURIFERA) 307
FRINGES 108–110
FROG 379, 380
FRUIT TREE 334 (*use for all varieties of fruit trees, and colour accordingly; could also represent 'tree of life' in Garden of Eden*)
FUNERAL BIER 50 (*omit body but use outline*)

G

GABRIEL see ANGEL OR MESSENGER
GALL (PAPAVER SOMNIFERUM) 313
GAMALIEL 88
GARDEN 439 (*Garden of Eden, Easter tomb, Gethsemane, Mount of Olives; tomb 415 fits into dots*)

GATHERING STICKS 261 (*replace corn by sticks*)
GEHAZI 148
GESHEM 71 (*fits waist 75*)
GIDEON 138 (*place trumpet 198 reversed in right hand and jar 221 or torch in left hand*)
GIRDLE see BELT
GIVING DRINK AT WELL see WOMEN AT WORK
GLADIOLUS (GLADIOLUS ILLYRICUS) 310
GLEANING 261
GNAT 381
GOAT 401
GODDESS DIANA 433
GOLDEN CALF 389
GOLIATH 189 (*for shield bearer, place 187 in front of Goliath's right foot and draw rectangular shield 20 cm high over right arm replacing sword*)
GOOD SAMARITAN STORY ass 386; Levite 107; priest 105; Samaritan 152; wounded man 54 (*fits ass 386*)
GOVERNOR 167
GRAPE VINE see VINE (VITRIS VINIFERA)
GREEKS citizen 170; orator 168; slave girl 173; widow 172; women 171–174; worker 169
GREETING 58, 59
GRINDING CORN 250
GUARD (ROMAN/PRETORIAN) 184
GUEST CHAMBER 407

H

HAGAR 64, 65
HAMMER 235
HAMPER see BASKETS
HANNAH 141
HAPPY see FACES
HARP see MUSICIANS AND MUSICAL INSTRUMENTS
HAY CART 300
HEADDRESS 93, 94 (*yard square of white linen folded diagonally and worn in various ways; men fixed it with black wollen cord, women draped it—see 95–99, 102*)
HEALING (JESUS) healing eyes, ears 27 (*use with 28, 29*); laying on hands 24 (*use with 41, 137; sits on foal 386*); raising 25 (*use with 47–50*); touching 26 (*use with 31–33, 37, 42*)
HEAVENLY HOST see ANGEL OR MESSENGER

HEBREW SOLDIER 183
HEN see BIRDS
HERBS AND SPICES anise, dill or fennel—Anethum Graveolens 304; frankincense—Boswellia Thurifera 307; hyssop—Origanum Maru 306; mustard—Brassica Nigra 302; myrrh—Cistus Creticus 305; myrtle—Myrtus Communis (*scented leaves*) 308; (*used to build booths for Feast of Tabernacles*); spikenard—Nardostachys Jatamansi (red) 303 (*perfume comes from hairy part of stem; imported from India*)
HEROD 153
HEROD'S TEMPLE see TEMPLE (HEROD'S)
HEZEKIAH (KING OF JUDAH) 162
HIDING 73
HIDING FACE 70
HIGH MOUNTAIN 437, 438
HIGH PRIEST 106 (*white linen shirt, mitre and embroidered sash worn by Priests and Levites; High Priest wore blue fringed tunic, embroidered ephod and breastplate over shirt*)
HIGH SOUNDING CYMBALS 202
HILL 436
HILL TOWN (BETHLEHEM) 414
HILLSIDE hill or mountain 436 (*raise skyline for Mount Carmel, Temptations, Beatitudes and teachings*); meeting place or camp 437 (*use desert well 411, tent 420 or as general country or desert background, enlarging to size required*)
HITTITES 186
HOEING 192
HOLY OF HOLIES 423 (*behind curtain at top of far steps*)
HORSE 398 (*fits shaft of chariot 299; use rider 21, omitting upper leg*)
HORSE FLY 384
HOUSE Palestinian house 408 (*enlarge and use for healing of paralytic, removing dome to let down bed*); poor dwelling 406 (*use for Israelite houses in Egypt; for Passover, enlarge to fit doorposts 62*); raised level 405 (*for interior living area, enlarge and use women 247–251*); rich dwelling 407 (*for upper room, Elijah's room, Jairus's house, Bethlehem inn*)

HULDAH (PROPHETESS) 141
HUSBANDMAN 86
HUSK locust bean 342 (*grows on carob tree—Ceratonia Siliqua; dried and fed to cattle and swine but edible by humans; nutritious*); cross section of pod 343 (*shows skin, flesh and bean*)
HYSSOP (ORIGANUM MARU) 306

I

IDOL OR IMAGE 432
INK POTS see SCRIBE
INN 407
INNKEEPER 87
INSECTS see PLAGUES
INSIDE OF HOUSE see HOUSE
IRIS (IRIS PALAESTINA) 309
ISAAC boy 143; for sacrifice on stone altar, 434, 150, 54; old age 149
ISAIAH 149
ISHMAEL 143
ISHMAELITES 93, 94, 404
ISRAELITES (CROSSING RED SEA AND WANDERING) 80

J

JACOB dreaming 52; old age 151; running 76; wrestling 56; youth 136
JAILER 169
JAIRUS 89
JAIRUS'S DAUGHTER 47, 144
JAR see POTTERY
JAVELIN 77
JEALOUS 65
JEERING 65 (*also see FACES*)
JEHOASH 143
JEHOSHEBA 165
JEPTHA'S DAUGHTER 63
JEREMIAH 151; in the well 73
JERICHO see CITY (ON HILL WITH WALL)
JERUSALEM street 409 (*also see CITY (ON HILL WITH WALL)*)
JESUS boy 143; asleep in boat 53; at baptism 3; at Last Supper 9; blessing bread 8; breaking bread 10; calling disciples 6; calling Zacchaeus 5; feeding of five thousand 11; hands outstretched 1; healing, see HEALING; praying in garden 51; preaching 22, 23; stilling storm 7; teaching, see TEACHING; teaching from boat 18, 23; walking to Emmaus 22; washing disciple's feet 13; waving 2; with children 4

INDEX

Index ...

JETHRO 105
JEZEBEL 165
JOHN MARK 85
JOHN THE BAPTIST 92
JONAH 138
JONAH'S SHIP 296
JONAH'S WHALE 376
JONATHAN 136
JORDAN 435
JOSEPH OF ARIMATHAEA 88
JOSEPH (NT) 152
JOSEPH (OT) boy with long-sleeved coat 137; in Egypt 176
JOSEPH'S BROTHERS 67, 68, 81–83
JOSEPH'S SILVER CUP 215
JOSHUA 152
JOSIAH 136
JOYFUL 63
JUDAS ISCARIOT kissing Christ 58; with money bag 148
JUGLET 211
JUMPING FOR JOY 34 (adapt as necessary)
JUNIPER BUSH/DESERT BROOM (RETAMA RAETAM) 323

K

KILLING 69
KILT 84
KING Ahab sulking 55; of Assyria 160; of Babylon 161; Herod 153; of Israel and Judah 162; of Persia 159; on throne 159
KISSING 58
KNEADING DOUGH 249

L

LABAN 152
LAD 84

LAKE 435 (enlarge at least double and use with boats 294, 295 and fishermen 279–284)
LAMB 395
LAME 30, 32
LAMP 104
LAMPSTAND 428
LAST SUPPER use figures 13, 15–17
LAUGHING see FACES
LAVER (BRONZE) 426
LAWYER 89
LAYING ON HANDS see HEALING (JESUS)
LAZARUS 82, 50
LEADING SHEEP 258
LEAH 140
LEPER begging and calling out 42, 43; cleansed, showing himself 45; Moses before Pharaoh 46 (join dots to bring out leprous hand); ringing bell 44
LETTING-DOWN NETS 280
LEVI/MATTHEW 286
LEVITE 105
LILIES OF THE FIELD anemone/lily—Anemone Coronaria 314; crocus/saffron—Crocus Sativus 316; cyclamen—Cyclamen Periscum 315; gladiolus—Gladiolus Illyricus 310; Iris/lily—Iris Palaestina 309; Narcissus Tazetta 311; opium poppy/gall—Papaver Somniferum 313 (gall is juice of poppy added to wine, including sleep); scarlet martagon/lily—Lilium Chalcedonicum 312
LION mouth shut 400; fierce face 402 (fits 400)
LISTENING at school 246; seated 20, 21
LOAVES AND FISHES 147
LOCUST 383
LOCUST BEAN see HUSK
LOINS GIRDED 83
LOOKING 71 (fits waist 75); 72
LOOKING UP TO HEAVEN (JESUS) 3
LOST SHEEP 395
LOT 152
LOUD CYMBALS 201
LYDIA 174
LYING DOWN dreaming 52 (fits whale 376 for Jonah); on couch 55; slain or robbed 54 (fits ass 386); sleeping 53; weeping 51
LYING ON BED corpse 50 (body or bier optional); Jairus's daughter 47; Peter's mother-in-law 49; paralytic 48
LYRE 208

M

MAGI 154
MAID 144 (of Naaman's wife)
MAIDENS 179, 180 (of Egyptian princess)
MAN ON FACE 57
MANASSEH (KING OF JUDAH) 162
MANGER 242
MANTLE 100, 101 (encloses hair; worn under headdress)
MARKET 229, 231 (repeat with different goods)
MARTHA 103
MARY Magdalene 102; mother of Jesus 139; sister of Martha and Lazarus 20, 63; wife of Cleopas 140
MATTHEW/LEVI 286
MATTRESS (ROLLED UP) 36
MENDING NETS 281
MEPHIBOSHETH 30
MERCHANT 229
MESHACH 82
MESSENGER see ANGEL OR MESSENGER
MIRIAM 144
MITRE (PRIEST'S HAT) 105–107
MONEY see COINS
MONEYCHANGER 231
MOSES baby 245; before Pharaoh 46; escaping 76; killing Egyptian 69; prince 176; older 90, 151
MOSQUITO 385
MOTHER AND BABY 241, 243
MOUNT OF OLIVES 439
MOUNTAIN, MOUNTAIN PASS see HILLSIDE
MOURNERS 57, 66, 70
MOUSE 382 (sits up or stands)
MULE see ASSES
MUSICIANS AND MUSICAL INSTRUMENTS cymbals 201 (loud); 202 (high sounding); drum 205 (Assyrian, played at waist); flute 204 (Egyptian); harp 206 (Assyrian); 208 (David's); 209 (Egyptian, played by priest); lyre 208; pipes 199; psaltery 207; shofar 198 (ram's horn trumpet, blown by priest); tambourine/timbrel 203; trumpet 198 (ram's horn), 200 (silver)
MUSTARD (BRASSICA NIGRA) 302
MYRRH (CISTUS CRETICUS) 305
MYRTLE (MYRTUS COMMUNIS) 308

N

NAAMAN 46
NAAMAN'S WIFE 141
NAAMAN'S WIFE'S MAID 144
NABOTH 87
NAOMI 141
NARCISSUS/ROSE (NARCISSUS TAZETTA) 331
NAZARETH 414
NEBUCHADNEZZAR (KING OF BABYLON) 161
NEHEMIAH 82
NICODEMUS 88
NOAH 149; sons 136–138; sons' wives 63, 139, 140; wife 141
NOAH'S ARK 293 (drawn to scale 1:590; front view shows raft-like structure on which three-storey building was made; length of ark was ten times height; this section is one-sixth of total length; repeat section between dotted lines eleven times before adding end reversed)
NOSE RING 101 (jewel rests on right cheek)
NURSING CHILD 243

O

OFFERING DRINK 253
OLD MEN 88, 148–150
OLIVE (OLEA EUROPAEA) branch 338 (fits beak of dove 361); cross section of olive 336; fruit and leaves 337; tree 339 (for Mount of Olives, draw several)
ONESIMUS 169
OPIUM POPPY/GALL (PAPAVER SOMNIFERUM) 313
ORPAH 140
ORTHODOX JEWS 108–110, 246 (distinctive features of clothing were fringed coat, length of fringe, prayer shawl/tallith and phylactery); Pharisees 108, 109; phylacteries 108 (sections of law in boxes bound to forehead and arm); Rabbi 110, 246; Sadducee 109
OXEN see CATTLE

P

PAINTING 62 (door posts and lintel for Passover)
PALESTINIAN HOUSE see HOUSE
PALM (PHOENIX DACTYLIFERA) date palm; fruit 350 (many such stalks grow in bunch) leaf 349 (detail shows leaves growing); stylised branch 351 (total length 2 m; can be held by figures 62, 138, 143–5, 147, 149, 168, 169, 174, 244); tree 348 (grows to 5 m)
PALSY 48
PAPYRUS/BULRUSH (CYPERUS PAPYRUS) 322
PARALYTIC (SICK OF THE PALSY) cured, taking up bed 34; four friends carrying man 35; lying on bed 48
PASSOVER (PAINTING DOORPOSTS) 62
PATH (THROUGH RED SEA) 440 (crowd 80 fits path)
PAUL 170
PAUL'S SHIP/ROMAN CORN GALLEY 297
PEN see SCRIBE
PENINAH 65
PETER denial 81; mother-in-law, sick with fever 49; preaching 151; walking on water 84
PHARAOH 178
PHARAOH'S DAUGHTER 181
PHARISEE see ORTHODOX JEWS
PHILEMON 170
PHILIP 82
PHILISTINE SOLDIER 187
PHOENICIAN TRADING VESSEL/JONAH'S SHIP 296
PHYLACTERIES see ORTHODOX JEWS
PIG swine 399 (for herd, duplicate several times)
PIGEON/ROCK DOVE 359
PILATE 167
PILATE'S WIFE 174
PINE OR FIR (ALEPPO PINE, PINUS HALEPENSIS) branch 345; tree 344 (grows to 20 m)
PIPES 199
PITCHER 220
PLAGUES frog 379, 380 (plague two); gnat 381 (plague three); horse fly 384 (plague four); locust 383 (plague eight); mosquito 385 (plague three)
PLATE 213
PLOUGH 263
PODS see HUSK
POPPY/GALL (PAPAVER SOMINIFERUM) 313
PORTICO see TEMPLE (HEROD'S)
POT 217
POTIPHAR 175
POTIPHAR'S WIFE 182
POTTER 223

POTTERY beaker 214; bowl 212; bushel 218 (two gallons); cup 215 (use for Joseph's silver cup); cup 216 (in general NT use); flask 210; jar 221; jar with handle 222; juglet 211; pitcher 220 (for carrying water, see WOMEN AT WORK); plate 213 (would have dip at centre to drain off fish oil); pot 217; stone jar 219 (twenty five gallons; used for wine at Cana wedding); (all drawn approximately one-quarter actual size)
POURING LIQUID 193
PRAYER SHAWL see ORTHODOX JEWS
PRAYING Jesus in garden 51; Jewish stance 61
PRETORIAN GUARD 184
PRIEST 105 (see also) HIGH PRIEST
PRINCE Egyptian 176
PRISCILLA 171
PRODIGAL SON 58, 59, 136
PROPHET 90, 149
PROPHET OF BAAL 67, 68, 200
PROPHETESS 141, 142
PSALTERY 207
PULLING-IN BOAT AND NET 279, 284 282
PULLING STONE ON SLEDGE 191
PURSE 276

QR

QUAILS (18 cm long) 367–369
QUARRELING 67, 68, 65
QUEEN Esther 164; Jezebel 165; of Sheba 163; Vashti 166
RABBI reading scroll 110; teaching 246
RACHEL 63
RAHAB 140
RAISING 25
RAM 393
RAVEN see BIRDS
READING (IN SYNAGOGUE) 110
REAPING 260
REBEKAH 139, 253
RED SEA 440
REEDS (PHRAGMITES COMMUNIS) 321
RESURRECTION APPEARANCES 1, 2, 10
RETURN OF PRODIGAL SON 58, 59
RHODA 173
RICH YOUNG RULER 89

INDEX

RIVERSIDE 435 (use for Jordan, Red Sea, Nile; alter width of water, move shore lines nearer together or farther apart; add papyrus rushes 322 near first bank for Moses in bulrushes)
ROAD (JERUSALEM TO JERICHO) 438
ROBBED MAN 54
ROBBERS 67, 68
ROMANS citizens 170; governor 167; women 171–173, 174
ROSE/NARCISSUS (NARCISSUS TAZETTA) 311
RUNNING AWAY 76
RUSHES (JUNCUS EFFUSUS) 320
RUTH 63, 261

S

SACK OF GRAIN 278 (Benjamin's sack)
SACRIFICIAL LAMB 395
SAD 64 (also see FACES)
SADDUCEE see ORTHODOX JEWS
SAFFRON/CROCUS (CROCUS SATIVUS) 316
SAILORS 84, 86
SAMARIA 412
SAMSON 82
SAMUEL adult 60; boy 54, 143, 146
SANBALLAT 67
SANDALS 81
SAPPHIRA 172
SASH see HIGH PRIEST
SARAH 141
SATRAP (PERSIAN OFFICIAL) 200
SAUL King of Israel 162; of Tarsus 82; on Damascus road 89; throwing javelin at David 77
SAW 240
SCALES 230
SCARLET MARTAGON/LILY (LILIUM CHALCEDONICUM) 312
SCHOOL 246
SCORPION 378
SCRIBE 228 (on table are ink, pots and pen, stylus, wax tablets)
SCRIP (OR WALLET) 275 (had shoulder strap and was carried by shepherds and travellers; held two days' food)
SCROLL/DECREE/EDICT 224, 225 (fits hands of Roman guard 184); rolled and tied for carrying Book of the Law 226, 227
SEA OF GALILEE 435

SEA (ROUGH) 298 (repeated for frieze)
SELLING 229
SENNACHERIB (KING OF ASSYRIA) 160
SEPULCHRE see TOMB/SEPULCHRE
SERPENT/SNAKE 377 (for Moses's pole, join dots and extend, stand vertically)
SERVING MAIDS 252–255
SEWING 248
SHADRACH 81
SHAWL see HEADDRESS
SHEAF 328
SHEEP ewes 394, 396 (for whole flock repeat, reversing and grouping); lamb or lost sheep 395; ram 393 (fits thicket 323)
SHEEP FOLD 256 (also see SHEPHERD)
SHEET (DRESSED IN) 85
SHEKEL 288
SHEPHERD carrying crook 258; carrying sheep 257; leading sheep (use sheep 394 repeated); sleeping in doorway of sheepfold 256; watching flocks 152, 257
SHIELD BEARER 187
SHIPS Jonah's ship, Phoenician trading vessel 296; Paul's ship, Roman corn galley 297
SHIRT 81 (shirt or under-garment always worn, made by folding sheet of cloth in half, sewing up sides and leaving armholes or inserting sleeves; hole for head was cut later in shape required; sometimes decorated; money and valuables carried in front fold above belt); loins girded 83 (back hem pulled up between legs from front and tucked into belt); long shirt 82 (had long sleeves and cloth girdle); working shirt 81, 86 (could be cut away at neck, armholes and side seams for freedom of movement)
SHOES 86
SHOFAR (RAM'S HORN TRUMPET) 198 (blown by priest)
SHOOTING ARROW 75
SHORE 435
SHOUTING 68, 133
SHOWING HANDS (JESUS) 1
SHRUBS bramble/briar—Rubus Ulmifolius 318; desert broom/juniper—Retama Raetam 323 (use as thicket for ram 393); papyrus/bulrush—Cyperus Papyrus 322 (use base repeated

along river bank); reed—Phragmites Communis 321; rush—Juncus Effusus 320; thistle—Silybum Marianum 319; thorn/burning bush, stylised version 317 (omit flames for other uses)
SICK OF THE PALSY 48
SILVER TRUMPET 200
SIMEON 149
SIMON OF CYRENE 86
SINGING 61
SITTING 15, 18–21; at receipt of custom 286 (use with tax collector 285); by pool 40; in door of sheepfold 256; on donkey 243, 248 (reversed)
SKIN (FOR WATER) 277
SLAIN 54
SLAVES 169, 173
SLAYING 69
SLEEPING 53
SLIPPERS 83
SMILING see FACES
SNAKE/SERPENT 377
SNEERING see FACES
SOLDIERS Assyrian 188; Egyptian 177; Philistine 187; Roman/Pretorian guard 184 (to hold scroll 225, omit spear and shield); Roman centurion 185 (holds spear in right hand); Syrian and other tribes 186
SOLOMON 162
SOLOMON'S TEMPLE 422
SOWING 262
SPARROWS see BIRDS
SPIKENARD (NARDOSTACHYS JATAMANSI) 303
SPINNING 251
SPY 72
STABBING 69
STABLE 419 (enlarge and use with: calf 389, donkey 387, Joseph 152, manger 242, Mary 139 or 248 reversed)
STACKING BRICKS 197
STAFF 152
STEPHEN 81
STEWARD (EGYPTIAN) 175
STILLING STORM 7
STONE JAR 219
STONES (OR ROCKS FOR TEMPTATIONS) 438
SULKING 64
SYCAMORE FIG/MULBERRY FIG (FICUS SYCOMORUS) fruit and leaves 346; tree 347; (low, flat branches are easy to climb)
SYNAGOGUE 421

T

TABERNACLE no illustration but use: table of shew-bread 425; bronze laver 426; altar of incense 429; altar of sacrifice 430; Ark of Covenant (hidden) 431; Ten Commandments 427
TABLE OF MONEYCHANGERS 231
TABLE OF SHEWBREAD 425
TAKING-UP BED 34
TAMBOURINE/TIMBREL 203
TARES 327
TASKMASTER (EGYPTIAN) 194
TAX COLLECTOR 286 (use with booth 285)
TEACHING from boat 18, 23; Rabbi 246; seated 18, 19; standing 22, 23
TEMPLE (HEROD'S) beautiful gate 424 (left of picture); balustrade 424 (to keep out Gentiles); Court of Gentiles 424 (outside balustrade); Court of Priests 423 (between two sets of steps); Court of Women 423 (up to first steps); Holy of Holies 423 (beyond far steps); money chests/Treasury 423 (all around Court of Women); portico 424 (top of picture, where public sat); (423—use dots as hinge and reverse picture to complete doorway; place altar of sacrifice 430 centrally in Court of Priests just through doorway); (different parts of 424 can be enlarged and used separately)
TEMPLE (SOLOMON'S) 422
TEMPTATIONS (JESUS) 6, 26
TEN COMMANDMENTS 427 (draw two)
TENT (NOMADIC) 420 (fit in figures 18–20 and adapt; for camp, reduce size of tent and group several)
THICKET 323 (use desert broom and ram 393)
THIN COW 392
THIRTY PIECES OF SILVER 276 (use purse 276)
THISTLE (SILYBUM MARIANUM) 319
THOMAS 81
THORNBUSH 317
THREE MEN (ABRAHAM'S VISITORS) see ANGEL OR MESSENGER
THRESHING 264
THROWING JAVELIN 77 (or

replace by stones)
TIMBREL/TAMBOURINE 203
TIMOTHY 138
TODDLER 244
TOMB/SEPULCHRE inside 416 (enlarge double to take grave clothes 50); outside 415 (fits garden 439 in space marked)
TOMB CLOTHES 50 (remove covering and use body only)
TOOLS see CARPENTRY TOOLS
TOUCHING 26
TRADING 229, 231
TRANSFIGURATION 1
TREASURY see TEMPLE (HEROD'S)
TREE OF KNOWLEDGE OR LIFE 334
TREES see individual entries
TRUMPET 198
TUNIC see HIGH PRIEST
TURTLE DOVE 361

UV

UNDERGARMENT 81
UPPER ROOM 407
VALLEY 438
VASHTI (QUEEN) 166
VEIL bridal veil 98 (covered body and face); face veil 97; 'instant' veil made from headdress 99
VESSELS see POTTERY
VEST 91 (made of sheepskin and worn by shepherds over or under shirt)
VILLAGE 413
VINE (VITRIS VINIFERA) (free standing, most commonly grown this way; black shows old wood; new branches bear fruit if old ones are pruned back to main stem each year; fruit supported by poles); trained over a trellis 330; complete vine 329 (reverse left onto right and repeat top branch at other levels both sides)
VIRGIN (WITH LAMP) 104

W

WAILING 66
WAIST DRUM 205
WALKING along road 5, 45, 76, 89; on water 84
WALLET 275
WARMING (BY FIRE) 24
WATCH TOWER 417 (for vineyard)
WATCHING FLOCKS 152, 256–8
WATER CARRIER 277

WATER SKIN 272
WAVES 298
WAVING 2
WAX TABLETS 228
WEAVING 247
WEDDING GUESTS 89, 104
WEDDING VEIL 98
WEEPING 51, 57, 66
WEEPING ON MAN'S NECK 58
WELL country well 411; town well 410 (use with women 252, 254, 255)
WHALE (SPERM) 376 (length twenty metres; use 52 for Jonah—fits inside)
WHEAT see CORN (TRITICUM COMPOSITUM)
WIDOW Greek or Roman 172; of Nain 66; of Zarephath 141; son of widow of Nain 50; son of widow of Zarephath 150
WILDERNESS 438 (use for Temptation, John the Baptist, Sinai, Jericho road; replace left hand rocks with burning bush 317 or stone altar 434 for Noah's and Isaac's sacrifices; for Brook of Cherith, draw stream between rocks)
WINNOWING 259
WISE MEN 154
WITHERED HAND (MAN WITH) 37
WOMEN AT WORK carrying pitcher on head 252; on shoulder 255; drawing water 254; filling pitcher 254 (stands on well 395); grinding corn 250; kneading dough in dough trough 249; nursing child 243; offering drink 253 (fits waist 252); sewing 248 (also sits on ass 386, omit sewing); spinning 251; weaving 247
WORK BENCH 232
WORKER 81, 83, 86, 169
WORKING COAT 87
WORKING SHIRT 81, 86
WRESTLING 56
WRITING see SCROLL/DECREE/EDICT and SCRIBE

YZ

YOKE for man 195; for oxen 390
YOUNG FACE 111, 112, 115, 116
YOUNG MAN 135–138
ZACCHAEUS 286
ZECHARIAH 151
ZIPPORAH 63

Action poses

Jesus, disciples:
1–27

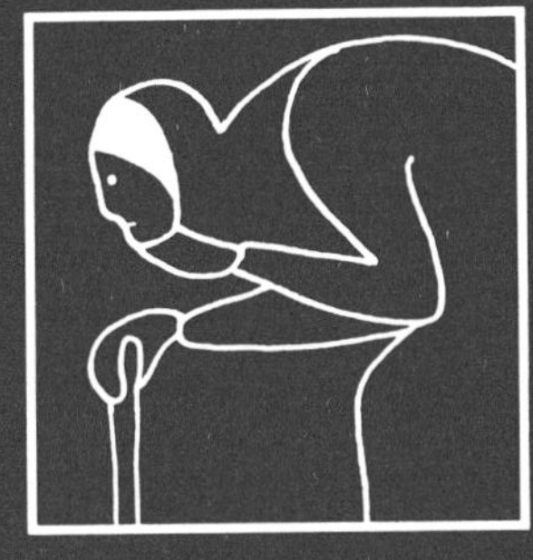

The sick, tired:
28–55

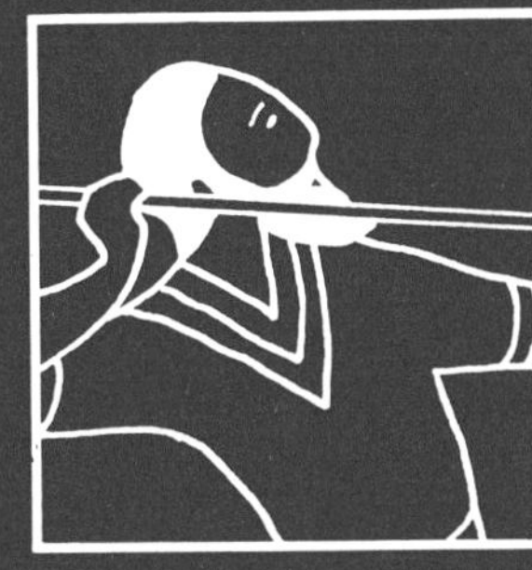

Acts, emotions:
56–77

Crowds:
78–80

1
2
3
ACTION POSES

4
5
6
7
ACTION POSES

8
9
10
11
ACTION POSES

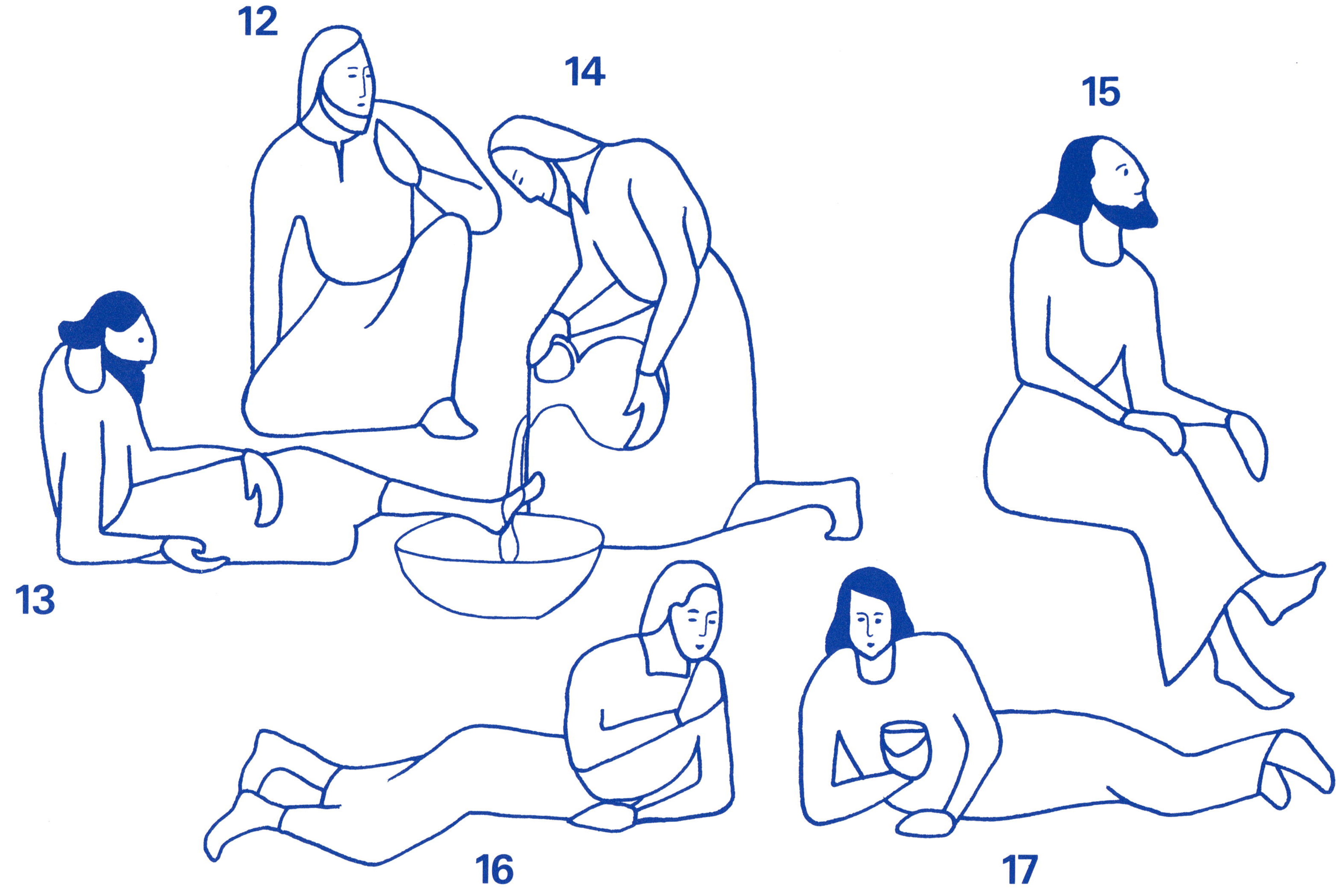

ACTION POSES

18
19
22
23
20
21
ACTION POSES

24
25
26
27
ACTION POSES

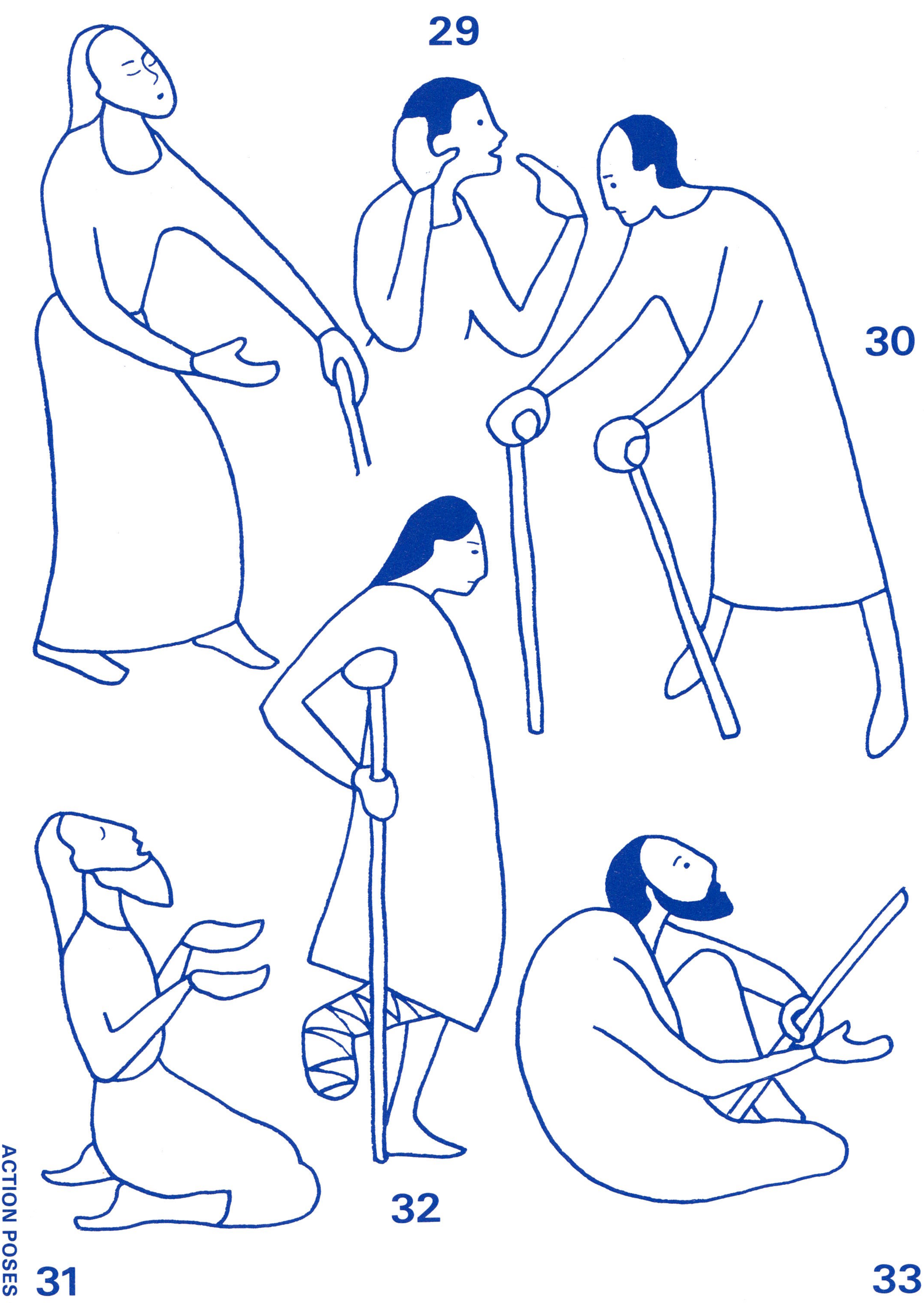

28
29
30
31
32
33
ACTION POSES

34
35
36
ACTION POSES

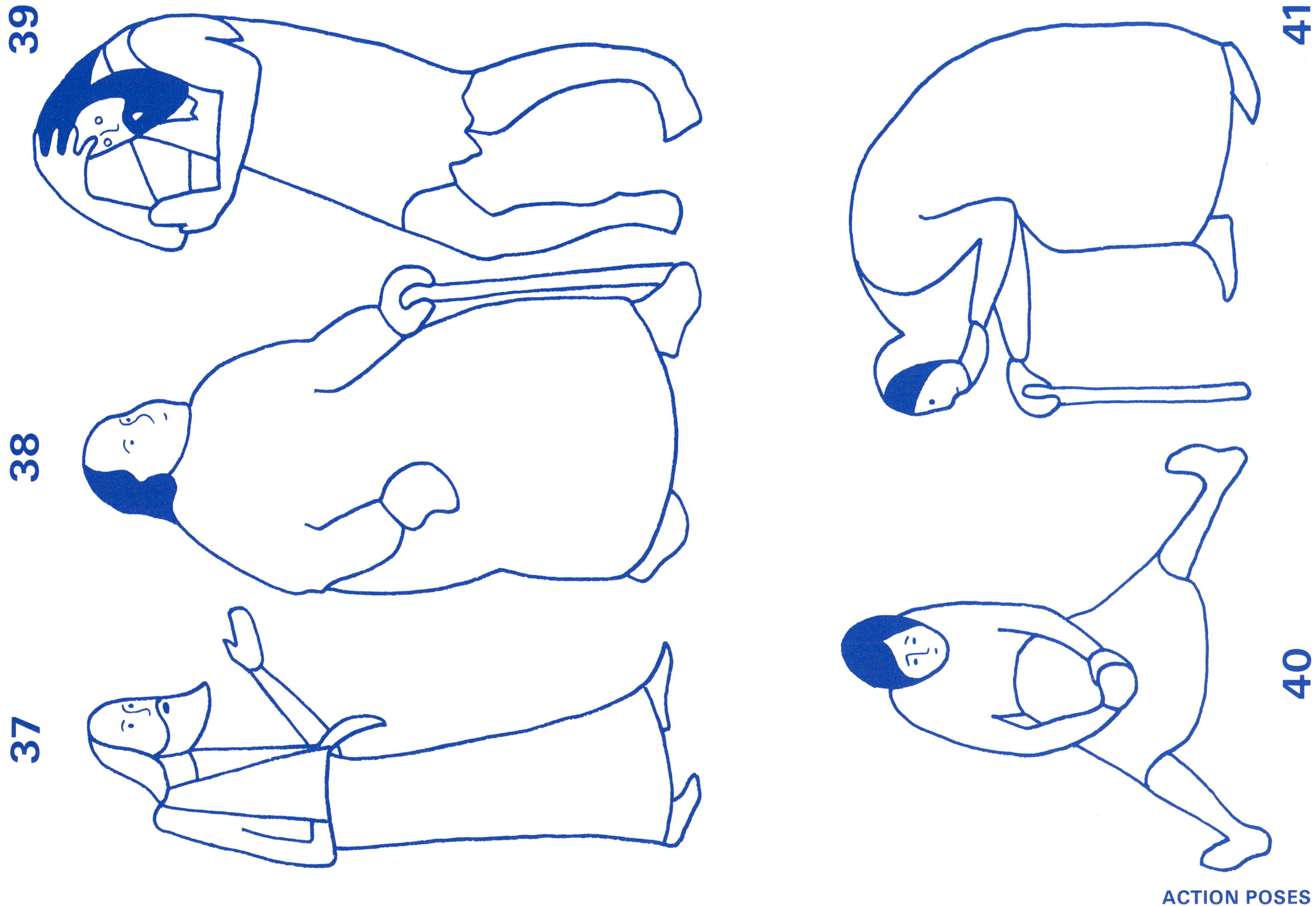

37
38
39
40
41
ACTION POSES

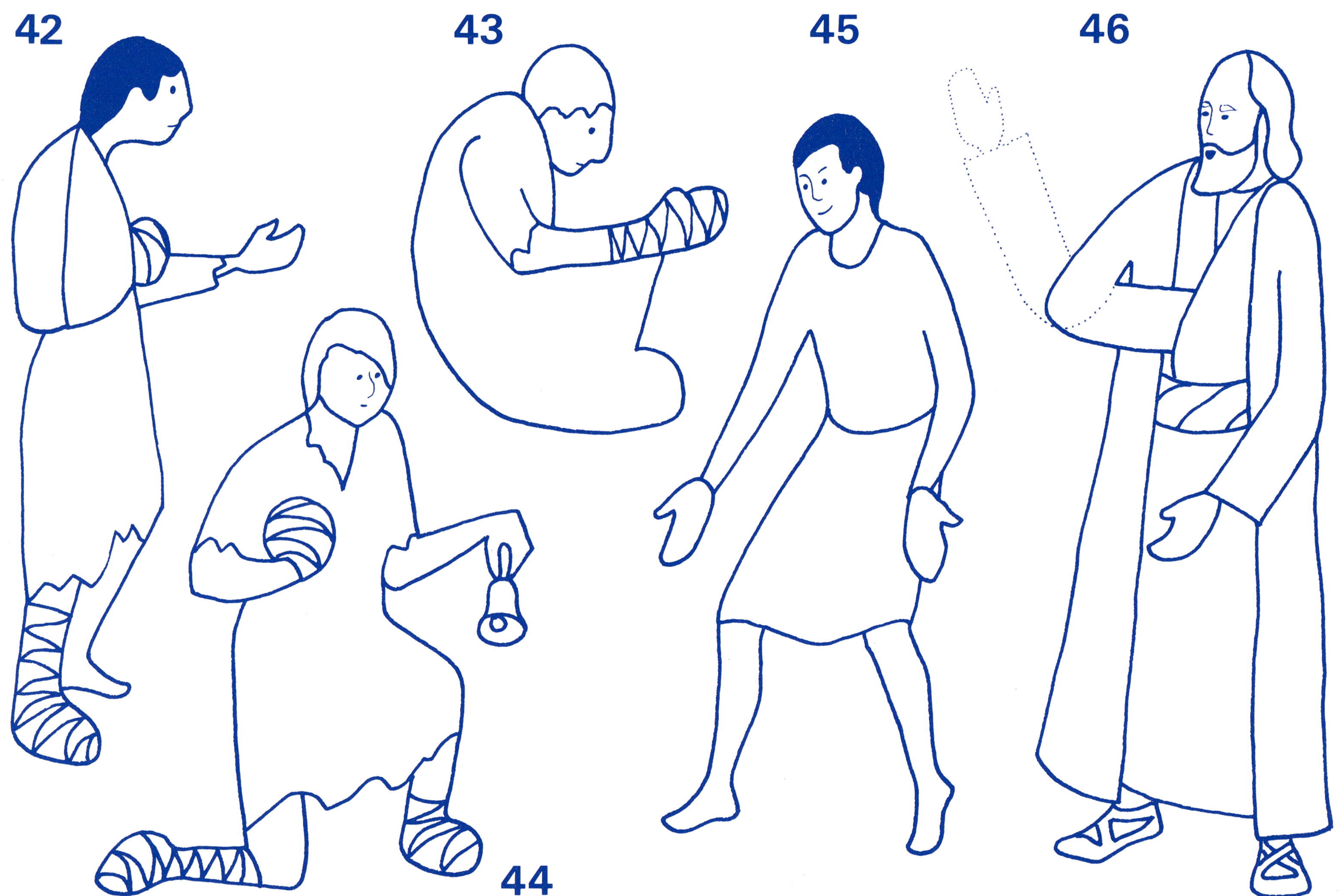
42
43
45
46
44
ACTION POSES

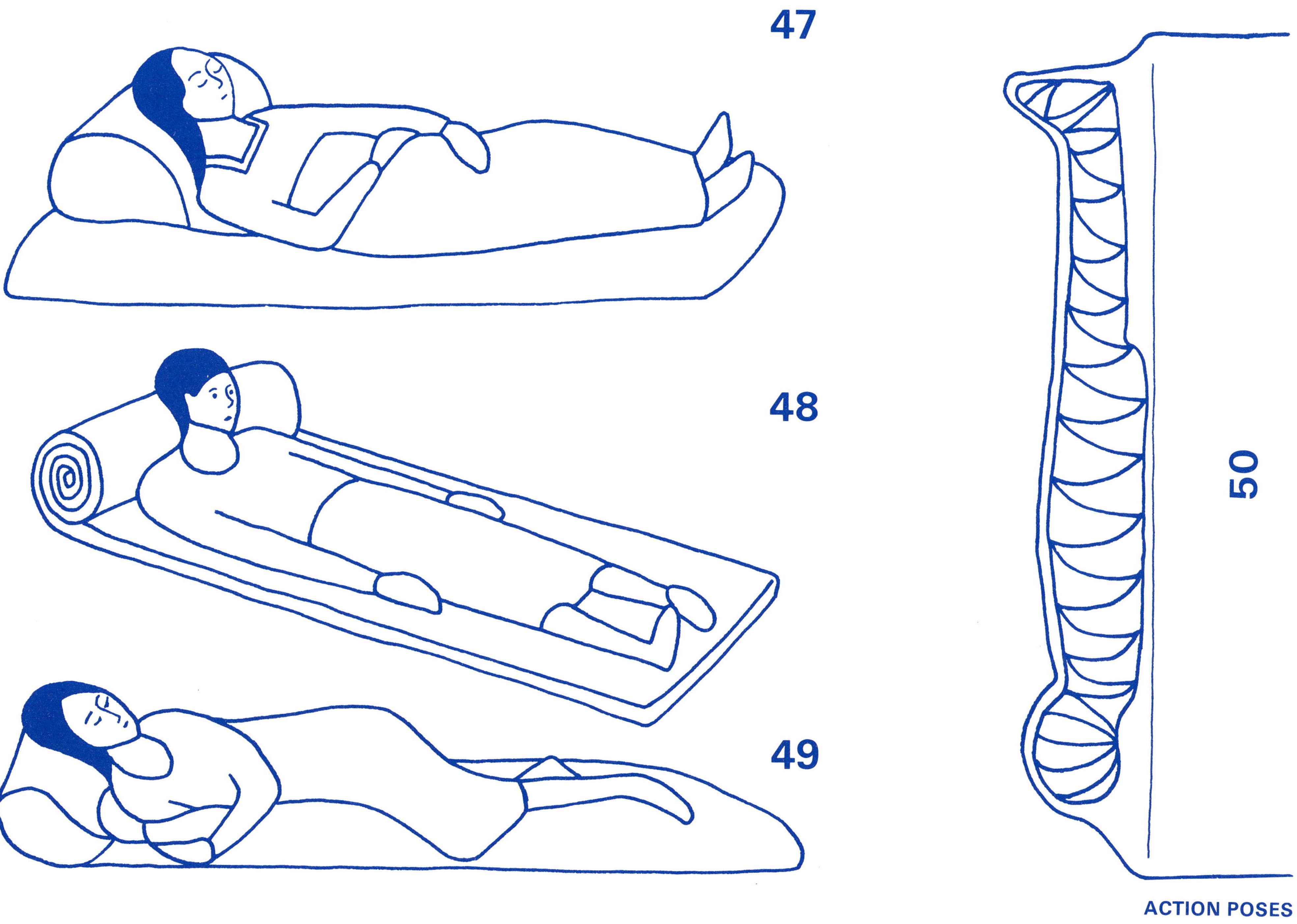

ACTION POSES

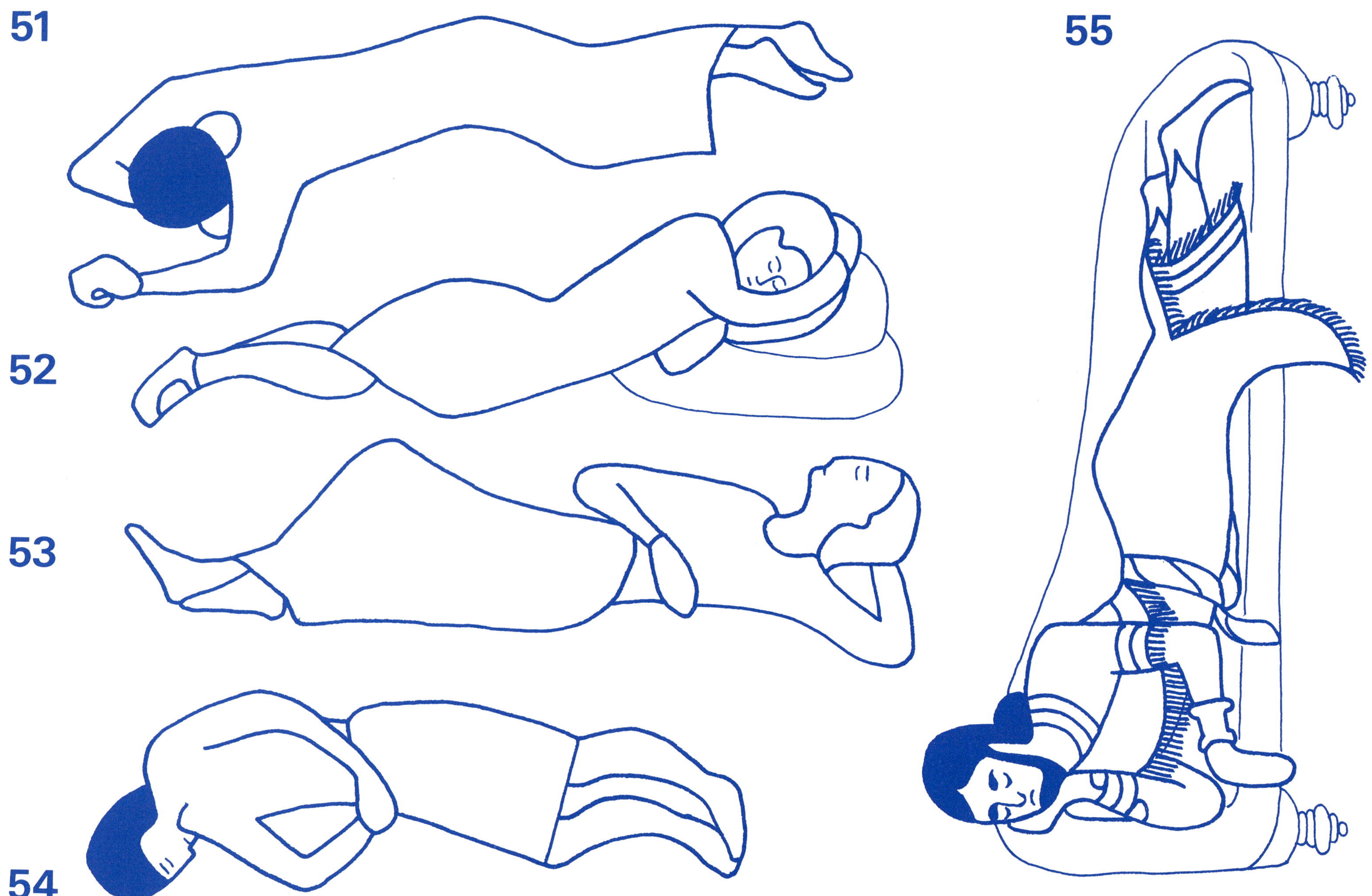

ACTION POSES

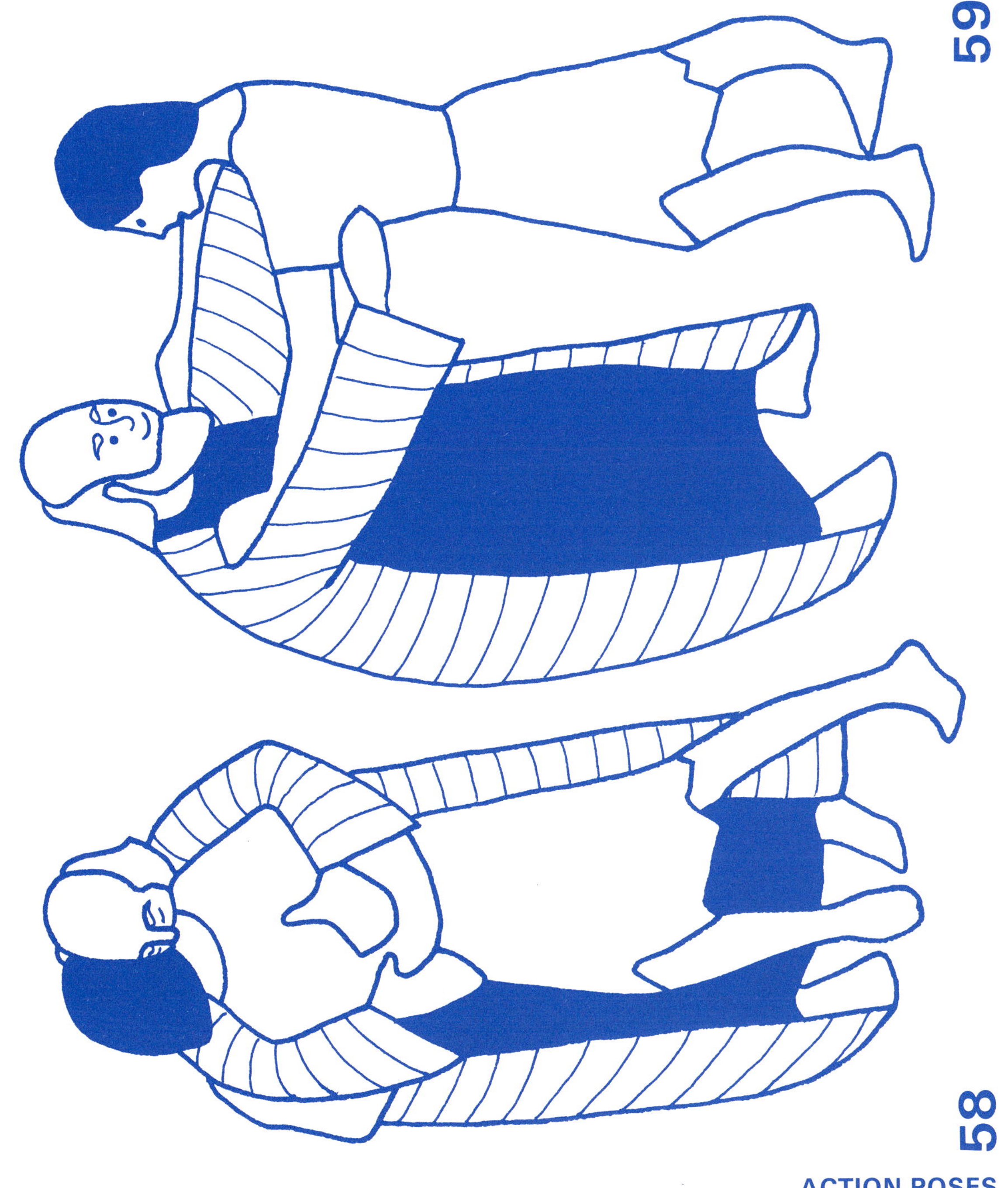

57
59
56
58
ACTION POSES

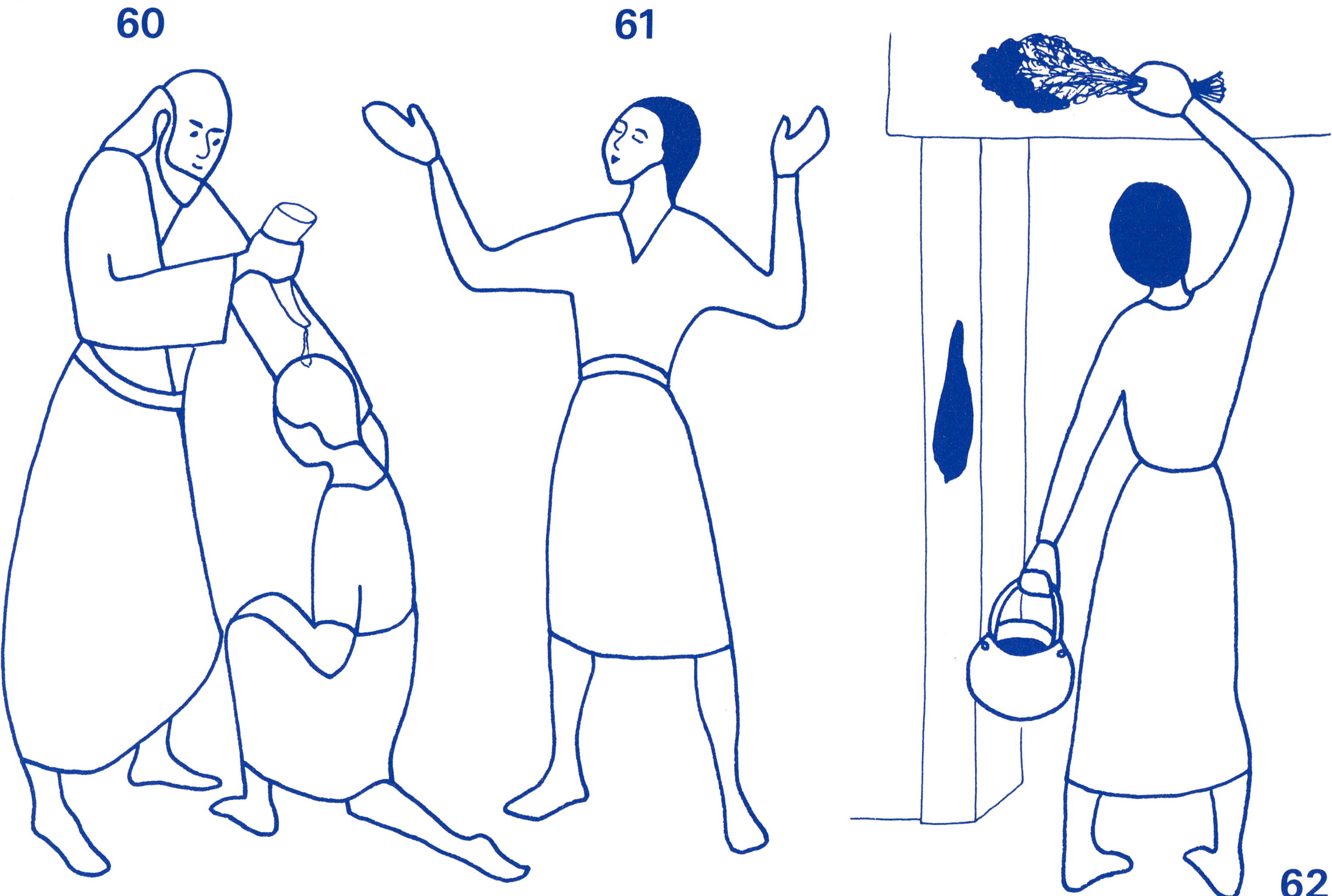

60
61
62
ACTION POSES

63
64
65
66
ACTION POSES

67
68
69
70
ACTION POSES

ACTION POSES

ACTION POSES

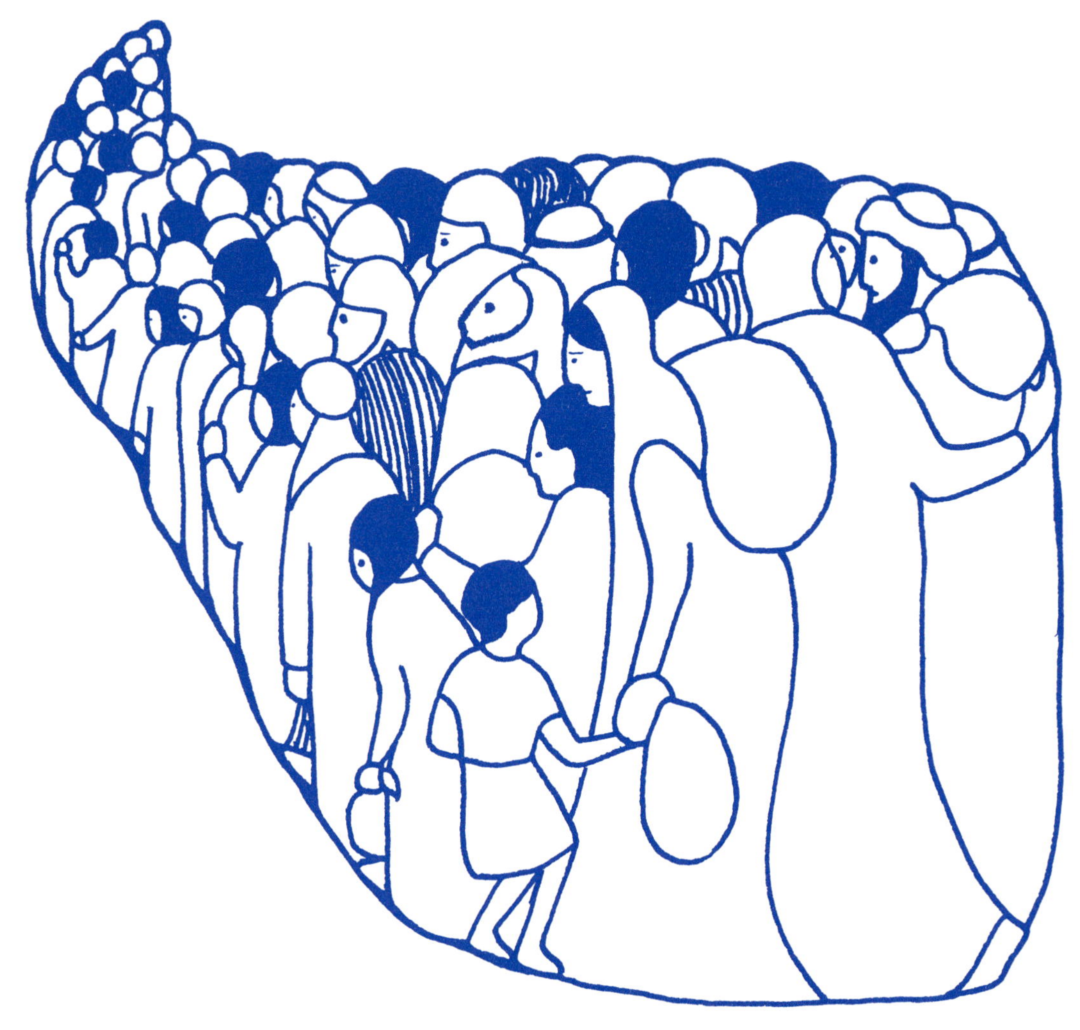

Clothes

Jewish costume:
81–110

81

82

83

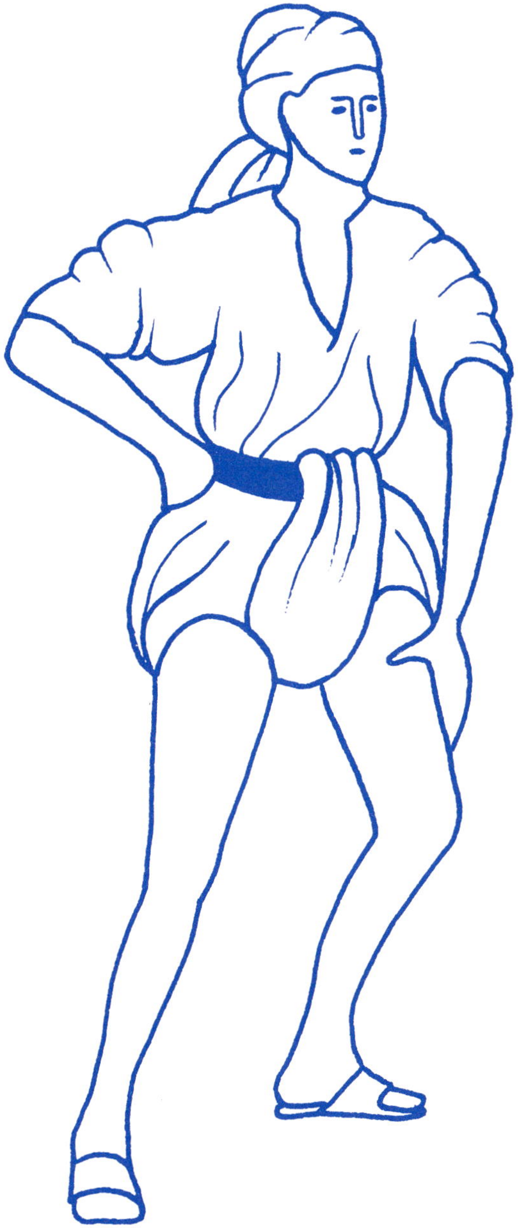

CLOTHES

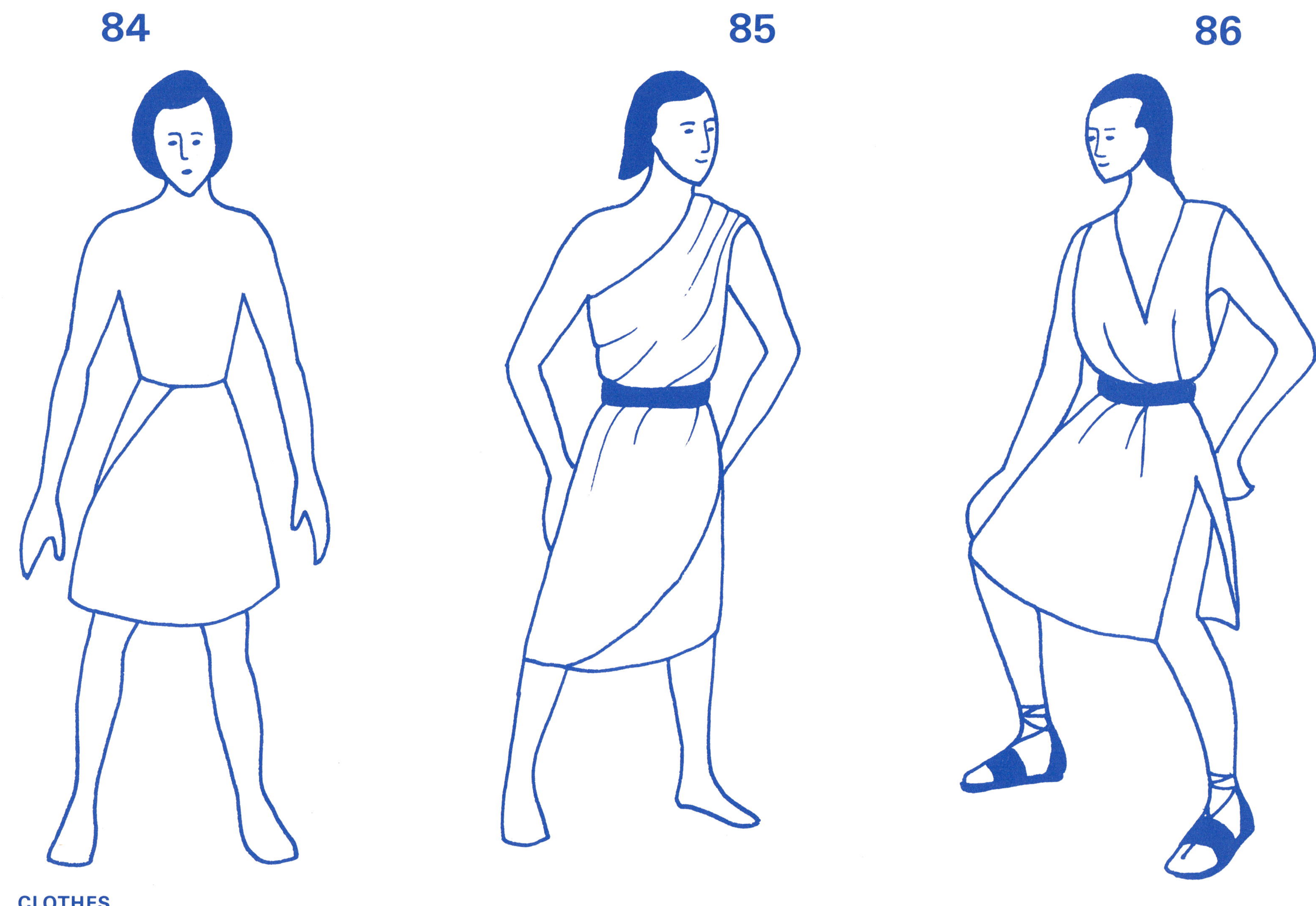

84
85
86
CLOTHES

87 
88 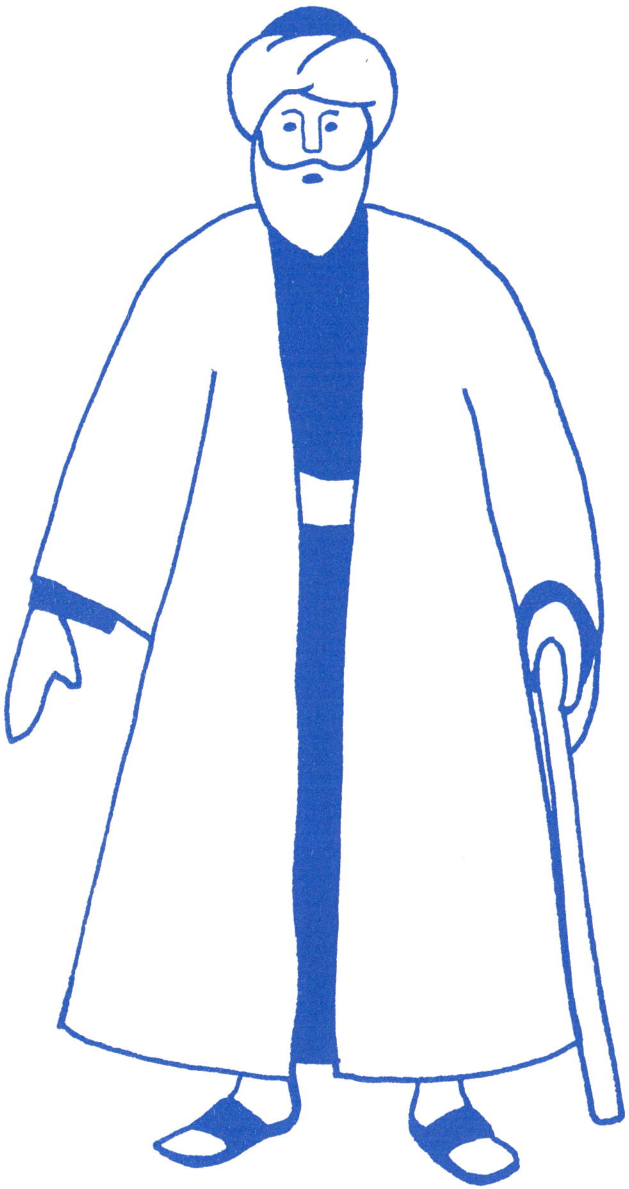
89
CLOTHES

90 
91 
92 
CLOTHES

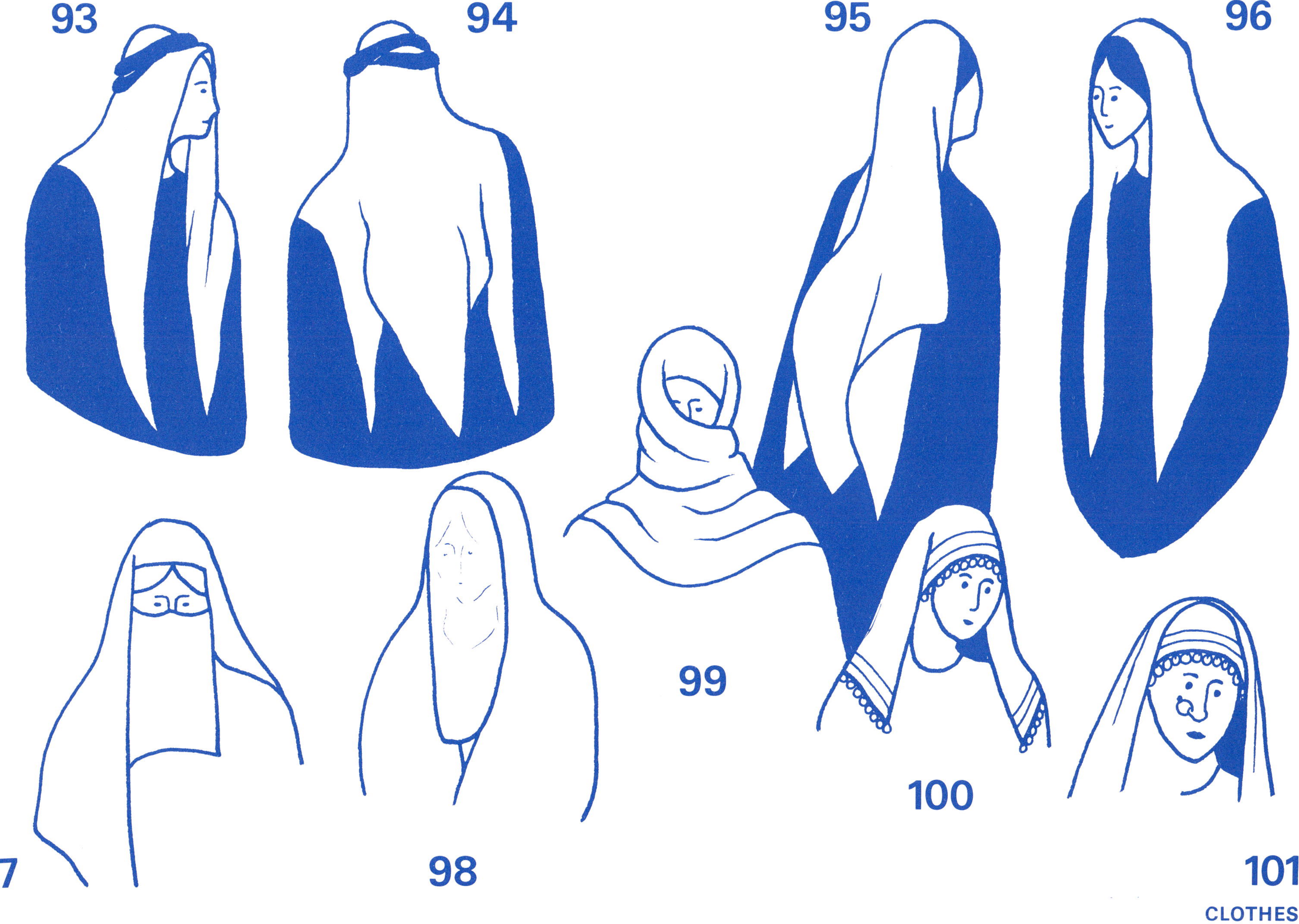

93
94
95
96
97
98
99
100
101
CLOTHES

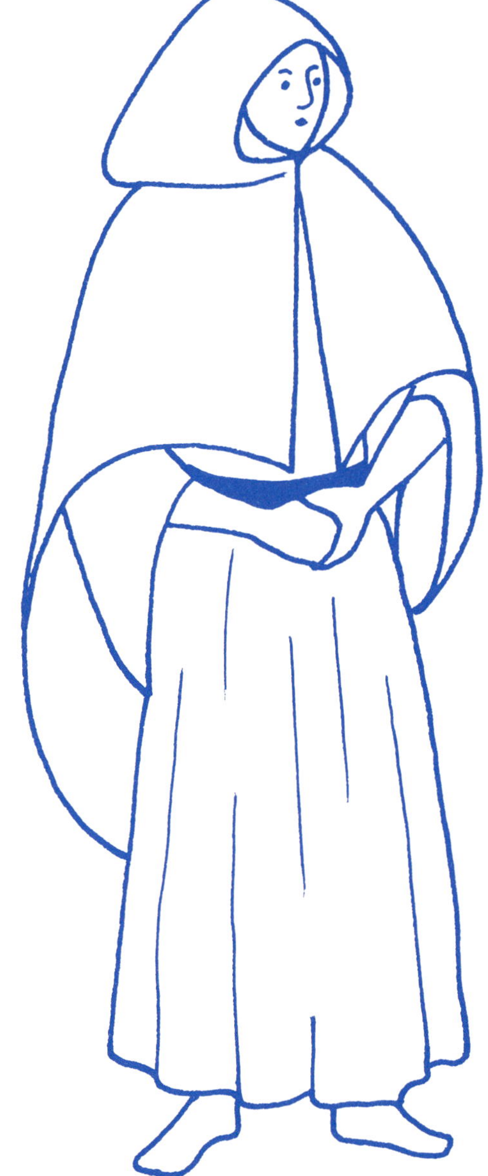

102

103

104

CLOTHES

105
106
107
CLOTHES

108
109
110
CLOTHES